DEATH AND ITS MYSTERIES

DEATH
AND ITS
MYSTERIES

Ignace Lepp

TRANSLATED AND WITH
AN INTRODUCTION BY
BERNARD MURCHLAND

The Macmillan Company, New York

Grateful acknowledgment is made to New Directions Publishing Corporation and to J. M. Dent & Sons Ltd., London, and the Trustees for the Copyrights of the late Dylan Thomas for permission to reprint from Dylan Thomas, *Collected Poems,* Copyright 1952 by Dylan Thomas.

Contents

TRANSLATOR'S INTRODUCTION: ix
    DEATH AND THE MODERN MIND

PREFACE   xvii

I ALL MEN ARE MORTAL 3

1 Physiological Death   5
2 The Experience of Death   8
3 The Death Instinct   17
4 The Scandal of Death   25

II THE FEAR OF DEATH 31

1 The Fear of Death Among "Primitive" Peoples   33
2 The Imaginary Anticipation of Death   35
3 The Death of Others   41
4 The Fear of Collective Death   46
5 Neurotic Fear   50
6 The Fear of Hell   53
7 Some Causes of the Fear of Death   56
8 Overcoming the Fear of Death   58

III   SUICIDE AND VOLUNTARY DEATH   67

1 The Temptation of Suicide   68
2 Cowardly Suicide   71
3 Neurotic Suicide   75
4 Blackmail and Suicide   81
5 Romantic Suicide   83
6 Mystical Suicide   87
7 A Tentative Psychological Explanation   88
8 The Right to Suicide   93
9 Voluntary Death   98

IV   DEATH AND LOVE   101

1 Romantic Death   102
2 Crimes of Love   108
3 Dying for Love of a "Cause"   110
4 Martyrdom   113
5 I Would Rather Die . . .   119
6 Love—the Conqueror of Death   121

V   THE MEANING OF DEATH   127

1 The Being-Toward-Death   127
2 Revolt or Distraction?   129
3 Choosing the Meaning of Life   133
4 Death in the Image of Life   139
5 The Death of the "Ordinary" Man   143
6 Death as the Fulfillment of the Person   145

VI   DEATH, WHERE IS THY VICTORY   152

1 The Human Reality   153
2 A Basic Intuition   155
3 The Immortality of the Soul   159
4 The Survival of the Soul: An Object of Faith   163
5 Spiritual Evolution   166

VII   IMAGES OF THE BEYOND   173

1 Experiences of the Beyond   174
2 Green Pastures   179
3 The Christian Paradise   182
4 Eternal Life   185

Translator's Introduction: Death and the Modern Mind

Do not go gentle into that good night.
Rage, rage against the dying of the light.
— DYLAN THOMAS

When a man has reached my age he ought
not to be repining at the prospect of death.
— SOCRATES

SECULAR man would seem not to think much about death. But in fact the thought of life's temporality looms ominously in the foreground of the modern consciousness. We live in the constant presence of the inevitability of death. We are haunted by the terrifying possibility of total extinction, insecure in our hope that something awaits us beyond the great divide.

Existential analyses, it may fairly be said, have contributed most powerfully to modern man's obsession with the subject of death. And Heidegger, discussed in the pages to follow, has furnished a typical and singularly astute thanatopsis. It was said in the past that philosophy was a preparation for death. It now seems to have become a discomforting form of death itself. On this view, death impregnates each of our choices with existential urgency. It does not lurk threateningly in the future but interpenetrates our present concerns and actions. Death embraces the whole of life; it is a mode of existence, a way of living. It is in fact life's greatest possibility and must be personally appropriated as such. All other responsibilities can be transferred or evaded or at least shared. But each of us faces death alone. How we do this determines the quality of our lives. Thus mortality is transcended by a free act of self-determination. We might recall Kierkegaard's anticipatory remark: "The inevitability of death accepted at the highest level of passion is an empowering thing." We might note, too, that the contemporary concern with death is most sharply focused in the "death of God" theology. The death of god is a common, indeed central, theme in the old mythologies. We think of Osiris, Attis, Adonis and Götterdämmerung. This myth seems always to be a way of emphasizing man's own mortality, of translating his fears and concerns at particularly crucial periods of history. It is one way, albeit a desperate way, of taking the sting out of death. By asserting that death holds sway over all things, that death is in fact a god, we purify our souls and paradoxically purge our memories of the horrible events of our century. The psychological technique involved here is not unlike the *katharsis* of Greek drama.

There is in this modern awareness something that is, if not precisely new, at least strikingly accentuated. It is, in the first place, an important aspect of the mood of the times. This mood can perhaps best be identified as the homelessness of man, his pervasive sense of alienation. A long litany of figures and diagnostic images could be easily summoned up to demonstrate the general sense of life's depreciation, the desolation of man's spirit in a desolate and desolating world. Secondly, contemporary discussion on the theme of death points to the radical need to reformulate the whole question. As Amos N. Wilder has perceptively observed: "The question of death and life beyond death has to be relocated today. Subtle changes have profoundly altered men's outlook and sensibility, and this affects even those who cherish traditional religious images. It is not only that terms like heaven and hell have to be put into quotation marks. Our sense of time has changed; we cannot so easily pass over the temporal in favor of the eternal. The very meaning of the ego or self has changed." (In Nathan Scott, ed., *The Modern Vision of Death,* p. 22) Furthermore, "Our confrontation with nothingness no longer waits upon the moment of death. Meaninglessness, vacancy, non-being has to be dealt with here and now. . . . Modern man is peculiarly naked to his limits, unassisted by those sentiments and idealizations which served as buffers for our fathers." (p. 23)

Dr. Ignace Lepp brings his experience and insights as a psychologist to bear upon this work of reformulation. He would be the last to claim finality or profundity for his efforts. Nonetheless he manages, in an easy yet evocative style, to open fresh perspectives on the ancient subject. I should like to single out two themes he dwells on for comment here. The first concerns his proposition that only by giving meaning to life can we give any meaning to death. This attitude has had a long history and finds classic illustration in the death of Socrates. The Socratic doctrine of the immortality of the soul was not a literal statement about religious belief. Rather, it was an avenue to peace of mind, a metaphor which symbolized that our life is not toward death but toward the good, toward the awakening of the soul in all men—which is to say an actualization of the fierce energies of the life process. It is in this sense that the soul "begets," that it is immortal. For a life devoted to the pursuit of meaning and goodness is a life devoted to perpetuating the awakeness of the soul, its self-consciousness and full existence.

We find the supreme expression of this in the way Socrates died. Death, which most men fear more than anything else, has no meaning for Socrates. It is merely a moment, not the end of life but its boundary, a horizon rather than a purpose. He is completely unrelated to death, and where despair and anxiety seem inevitable, there Socrates is full of the peace and loving wisdom that opens the soul. His only concern is to comfort those who have come to comfort him and set the example of how to die. He dispels the ambient grief and anguish with a jest. "Perhaps it would be better to bathe me now before taking the poison and so spare the women the trouble." By this bit of attention to the trivial he sets in relief the importance of living. He shows that he is not dying or fading away but that his death, like all other things in life, is merely a moment which has its time and place. In the *Apology* he reveals the sense of his total nature by reducing the significance of death to a syllogistic formula: "The state of death is one of two things: either the dead man wholly ceases to be and loses all consciousness or, as we are told, it is a change and a migration of the soul to another place. And if death is the absence of all consciousness, and like the sleep of one whose slumbers are unbroken by any dreams, it will be a wonderful gain. . . . But if death is a journey to another place . . . what good could be greater than this?"

Socrates' attitude has been imitated in various ways in the course of history. Death's sting has been stolen again and again in the name of life. Thus Romantic intensity, often enough a far cry from Socratic calm, sets itself against death's apparent victory. Walter Kaufmann offers a recent version of that way: "If one lives intensely, the time comes when sleep means bliss. If one loves intensely, the time comes when death is bliss. . . . The life I want . . . is a life of love and intensity, suffering and creation, that makes life worthwhile and death welcome." (*The Faith of a Heretic,* p. 372) Or the more sober tones of the atheist. Corliss Lamont, for example, says that the mature man is "not preoccupied with death; nor does he permit it, on account of the heartache and crisis it causes, to overshadow the other phases of human existence. . . . No, the wise man looks at death with honesty, dignity and calm, recognizing that the tragedy it brings is inherent in the great gift of life." ("Mistaken Attitudes Towards Death," *The Journal of Philosophy,* January 1965, p. 36) David Hume, in his *My Own Life,* speaks in a similar voice of his approaching death. He recounts how he was stricken with a "disorder in my bowels," how he calmly envisaged "a speedy dissolution," and concludes, "It is difficult to be more detached from life than I am at present." Finally, there have been various religious versions of the Socratic acceptance of death. Even the more naive and cruder forms of religious belief (expectation of reward in the hereafter, etc.) represent ways of diluting the horror of death by insisting upon life's worth. Faithful to this tradition, Lepp asserts the primacy of the life instinct and endeavors to reconstruct the meaning of death in terms of the life-giving values of love and knowledge. It is not how we die, he argues, but how we live that matters. Thus the issue is more the quality of life than the finality of death. In this way he shows how the modern preoccupation with death can paradoxically enhance life's creative possibilities. This is an important emphasis.

The second of Lepp's themes I want to elaborate upon is his hypothesis of creative evolution. The context here is Darwinian but Lepp seems primarily indebted to Henri Bergson (who first used the expression in his book of that title published in 1906) and the more spiritual contributions of Teilhard de Chardin. Bergson insisted that mechanistic and materialistic modes of explanation distort reality. If we think of the intellect and its concepts as fixed, static categories we cannot comprehend the richness and fluidity of the life process. Bergson noted that the most distinguished feature of our personal life is the constant change that is taking place in it. One state succeeds another in an unceasing flow. The self is pulsating, dynamic, and characterized by "centers of intensity" that make up the fabric of our experience. As such, the self is different from the realm of physical objects because it is growing, pushing on toward an end and thus forging its identity in history. Bergson found confirmation for his theory of evolution and growth in the biological order. There must, he argued, be an integrating force that gives living things organization and direction. He calls this force a cosmic vitalism, an *élan vital,* life itself. In the long course of evolution life strives to liberate itself from the dominion of matter and attain self-consciousness. Bergson distinguishes three phases in the evolution of the animate world. First, there is the vegetable kingdom. Secondly, there is the emergence of the arthropods, such as bees and ants, which are both mobile and instinctual. Thirdly, evolution resulted in the vetebrates and eventually man, who is distinguished by intellect and freedom. In this sense, man may be considered the end of evolution.

In his later period Bergson explicitly identified the primal energy of the universe as love and accepted the view of the Christian mystics that "God is love and the object of love."

Thus the divine is achieved in mystical experience. In this experience creation appears as "God undertaking to create creators, that he may have beings worthy of his love." Teilhard de Chardin recast a substantial part of Christian doctrine in light of Bergson's philosophy. It is, of course, far too early to judge the validity of this hypothesis. The twentieth century is not a convincing piece of evidence in support of any progress theory. Furthermore, there is much that is vague and ambiguous in both the vocabulary and the methodology of creative evolution systems. I am not in great sympathy with their Romantic overtones. The effort to exalt man by freeing him from his material environment can be a dangerous form of hubris. And the history of the West is strewn with the shambles of many Babels. A little more "naturalism," it seems to me, would be a desirable antidote, less insistence on how spirit can transcend matter and more on how it can more effectively utilize its sensuous media. Still, the Bergsonian synthesis is an attractive vision and as such constitutes an invitation to ponder life's secrets and relish its variety.

Lepp, at any rate, is able to illuminate the issues of death and immortality against the background of that synthesis and make the category of creativity the center of his speculations. He offers a viewpoint that permits us to interpret the spectre of death that haunts our century as one of the signs of the times by means of which we may better orient ourselves in life. That spectre speaks of the seed that must die to bear fruit; it reminds us of the immense labor that awaits us in building a human and cosmic world; it points undeniably to human capacity and energies; and, mutely but not altogether inaudibly, it holds forth the promise of a new form of faith in life.

BERNARD MURCHLAND

Preface

*We live and die alone;
no one can help us.*
—PASCAL

CAN we imagine a more universal human problem than death? Nor is there any danger that it will cease to be "current." It is not surprising that all the philosophers, all men capable of a minimum of reflection, have been more or less dramatically concerned with it and have felt obligated to make some pronouncement on it. Both religions and philosophies have proposed explanations for man's mortal condition and tried to elucidate its meaning and significance.

Like all men, I too have reflected on death in general and my own death in particular. When I was five years old I witnessed my grandmother's final agony and I remember it vividly. Over the years it has haunted my dreams. I was not especially fond of this austere and harsh old woman. If I wept with the other members of the family gathered about her deathbed it was undoubtedly less because I was sorry to lose her than because I was impressed by the mystery of death itself. Later, in adult life, I have seen many people die, many of whom were very close to me. Moreover, I have on several occasions found myself in situations where death seemed inevitable. It was only by a "miracle," or, if you prefer, by a happy chance, that I escaped its clutches.

But I did not decide to write a book on death because of my personal experiences. In fact I never thought about such a project at all and had in mind several books on quite different themes. But at the international symposium on Teilhard de Chardin, held in Bruges in 1964, the idea of a book on death impressed itself on my mind so forcibly that I felt obliged to set aside my other projects, many of them near completion, in order to consecrate myself totally to observation, study and meditation of the facts relevant to the problem, or rather to the *mystery,* of the ultimate act of human existence. Men and women from many countries and of diverse professional, intellectual and religious backgrounds attended that conference in 1964. We studied the different problems of the human condition in the exalting perspectives of Teilhard's cosmogenesis and noogenesis. My own contribution bore on the possibility of elaborating a new morality which would, certainly, be a "natural" morality but would take into account the fact that human nature is not something given once and for all but a task to be realized—a dynamic rather than a static task. I proposed a morality whose chief aim would not be the conservation of an immutable order of things but the promotion of human becoming toward an ever-increasing *spirituality.* Most of the participants shared these perspectives; they were very much in the spirit of our common master, Teilhard de Chardin. Nonetheless one of my friends, an eminent Belgian politician, said in a lecture:

"Your Teilhardian optimism in all of its cosmic, noogenetic

and communitarian aspects is very attractive but it neglects a fundamental fact, namely, the fact that we are all mortal. As soon as I mentally contemplate my own death I feel alone and abandoned, the prey of anguish. The essential problem for me then becomes not what the state of the universe or humanity will be in 1,000 years, but what awaits me personally on the other side of the great journey."

I could see many people in the audience nodding their heads in approval of my friend. His reservations impressed me, for he was a man of action, known as much for his dynamism as his zest for life. He was, moreover, a fervent admirer of Teilhard de Chardin. Wouldn't it be worth my while, I asked myself, to reflect further on a problem that was of great existential importance even for many of Teilhard's disciples? Perhaps I would be able to shed some light on it for them as well as for others. Everyone confronts the terrible fatality of death, which seems to doom everything we realize in the course of a lifetime to failure.

There are a good number of excellent books on the subject of death. There is, first of all, the work of physiologists who have attempted to establish the exact moment and symptoms of the passage from life to death. The importance of what science can teach us about the nature of the cells that make up our bodies, and especially our brains, is incontestable. They have much to say about the perpetual renewal of the cells, their aging process, the chances for their rejuvenation and the final disintegration of the "human composite"—that well organized city which is our body. But biology and physiology cannot answer the most agonizing questions men ask about death.

Other books, many of them of high spiritual value, have been written by philosophers and theologians. The latter contemplate death in the perspective of Christian revelation and theology. They accept the Christian teaching on earthly life, heaven, purgatory and hell as incontestable truths which they can only explicate in order to give death its full meaning and mitigate its agonizing aspects. As a matter of fact, many believers find in such books the comfort they need to accept life and death. I have often heard unbelievers, who have witnessed the serenity of their Christian friends, say that the latter are fortunate to be delivered from most of the enigmas of human existence which they encounter.

But today, even in traditionally Christian countries, the dogmas of Christianity are far from evident for increasing numbers of people. Moreover, many professed Christians who adhere intellectually to the teachings of the Church are anything but secure in their faith. They are often troubled by the materialism of the natural sciences, by the increasingly vertiginous dimensions of the known universe which make man and his problems appear insignificant. I doubt that the meditations of the mystics or the speculations of theologians on death can be of much existential help to such people.

Are the reflections of philosophers, who have meditated for centuries on the same mysterious problem, more illuminating? We shall have occasion to cite their writings. But we should bear in mind that the ancient philosophers dealt with the problem in a way that scarcely responds to the anguish of modern man. On the other hand, many contemporary philosophers, such as Berdyaev, Scheler, Lavelle and Marcel, adopt a fundamentally theological approach to death while others, like Heidegger and Sartre, merely note the irremediable absurdity of human existence since all effort inevitably terminates in death.

Yet it is impossible for the vast majority of men to live and act as though death did not exist, as some philosophers and moralists recommend. Whatever we do to forget it, we are repeatedly reminded that everyone must die. Those we love and admire must one day die. We are especially reminded of our own mortality. Nor is there much consolation in the hope for the eternal survival of the race as a whole. This used to be the hope of a certain kind of rationalist. Since the discovery and the destructive uses of thermonuclear energy, we know that men are in possession of a frightful instrument of collective suicide that could destroy mankind at any moment. It is not a question of an eventual collective suicide being willed by all men. We know that the folly of a small number would suffice to snuff out the whole race.

Whether we want to or not, we are therefore obliged to confront the problem and the mystery of death in all of its depth. Like the last years of the Hellenic era, the fall of the Roman Empire, the end of the Middle Ages and other periods of human history that were particularly catastrophic, our own age seems to me especially conducive to meditation on the mysteries of death. Nothing remains of the somewhat naive optimism of the nineteenth century when science and progress were expected to abolish all evils, both individual and collective. All traditional certainties are collapsing; cultures and civilizations are breaking up; humanity as a whole has become aware of the extreme precariousness of its existence.

In the chapters which follow, I shall approach the problem of death as a depth psychologist. The task of the psychologist here is not an easy one. There is no way of directly contacting the souls of the deceased, supposing that they continue to exist in one form or another. We will examine what the spiritualists and mediums have to say about the beyond; but we will have to recognize that their information tells us much more about themselves than about the deceased. The ontological content of their experiences is weak, indeed nonexistent. But they are not without psychological interest. Spiritualists, too, belong to the large family of those who will die, of men who are aware of their mortal nature. Given the fact that we cannot interrogate the dead, the answers we can obtain from those who know they are mortal will be of great interest for our purposes. Our observations and meditations will principally concern them. We propose to analyze the fear of death, which is a source of suffering for many men, paralyzing their zest for living and creating. Is there any way of overcoming this deep-rooted fear? Can death be meaningful? Is it possible to triumph over the fatality of death?

Are those who commit suicide, who deliberately choose death, cowardly or courageous? What conscious and, above all, unconscious motives push them to commit an irreversible act, one that precipitates them into the great unknown that so terrifies most men? Is there a basic psychological difference between those who commit suicide and those who sacrifice themselves for a "cause," such as martyrs? What are we to think of the intimate relationship that mystics and poets postulate between death and love? Can love be a cause, excuse or justification for death? Can we really die from an excess of love? And, finally, what are we to think of man's almost universal hope for immortality? What can we know or divine of such a possible state?

It goes without saying that psychological observations and experiences cannot furnish an adequate answer to all of these questions. As I said earlier, death is less a problem than a mystery. And only problems have solutions. Thus, in the pages that follow, I do not pretend to omniscience. I will be quite satisfied if I succeed in casting some light on the most profound and poignant mystery of the human condition.

The psychologist must, evidently, begin with the inner experience to which the techniques of his discipline give him access. He must remain as close as possible to this experience. But like any man of science he has the right, indeed the duty, to transcend experience. Teilhard de Chardin was criticized because he raised issues that cannot be verified experimentally, such as the culmination of the evolutionary process in a "divine milieu," the role of Christ in the evolutionary process, and the like. But what authentic scientist does not go beyond strict empiricism? Perhaps a laboratory assistant stays within such limits. But it is clear that humanity is not indebted to laboratory assistants for its remarkable conquest of the forces of nature and physical maladies. The genuine scientist interprets empirically observed facts and integrates them into a general system, into a synthetic vision of the universe. To be sure, one runs the risk of committing serious errors in constructing such a synthesis. This explains why so many theories, often contradictory, proliferate in the sciences. But there is no other available method and the immense progress realized by man as a result of scientific inquiry proves that this method is not altogether ineffectual.

For those who are not yet convinced of the psychologist's obligation to extend his reflections beyond the observable and verifiable, I would recommend reading of one of the most remarkable scientific thinkers of the younger generation, the physicist Jean Charon. Charon does not think he is unfaithful to his discipline because he talks about being and existence, creation and belief. And if it is permitted to the scientist to speculate and construct scientific theories which may at the same time have a philosophical and even mystical dimension, why shouldn't the psychologist have the right to meditate on those subjects, such as the life of the soul, which his discipline can illuminate? In the era of triumphant rationalism only logically secured truths were considered creditable. We now know the abuses to which this led. If one chose the terms of a proposition carefully enough he could prove anything at all— the existence or non-existence of God, the immortality or non-immortality of the soul. It was such rationalistic acrobatics that led Chesterton to say that the madman has lost everything but his reason. Long the exclusive property of rational logic, truth came to be considered accessible only to laboratory experimentation. Students of as recently as thirty years ago well remember such peremptory declarations as, "It is scientifically proven that. . . ."

I personally attach the utmost importance to logical reason and scientific experimentation, on condition that they are controlled by objectives they are capable of achieving. But other modes of knowledge, such as the poetical and mystical, are legitimate and normal as well. I do not consider these substitutes for scientific knowledge; they are mutually complementary. I deem the intellectual maturity of mankind sufficiently advanced to understand that the scientist must eschew all forms of doctrinal prejudices, that he must not reject those ways of gaining knowledge which are not verifiable in a scientific sense. To say, for example, that Teilhard de Chardin's theories on evolution are scientifically respectable but that his vision of the future of mankind is not, strikes me as an aberration. It indicates a radically mistaken notion of how the best scientists operate. Moreover, it ignores the fact that the most fundamental kinds of evidence are not "demonstrable" rationally at all, let alone by laboratory experimentation. This applies to our own lives, to the nature of the universe about us as well as the eventual survival of the soul after death. Philosophers who have tried to prove such basic issues rationally have ended with an absolute idealism that ends in universal doubt. Intuition, which plays a role in the human species comparable to that of instinct in animals, is alone capable of giving us an insight into those basic truths that the poets and mystics endeavor to communicate. Of course, the scientist must make every effort to verify intuitive knowledge by the specific methods of his discipline. His faith in intuition must never be blind.

Thus the psychologist cannot be blamed if his effort to illuminate the subject of death is no more successful than that of the biologist or the physicist. Our proposal to adhere as closely as possible to the data of inner experience forces us to go beyond that data. Particularly in discussing life after death, we will often be obliged to leave the level of the rational and experimental in order to profit by more intuitive modes of knowledge. In this matter we shall rely principally upon the inner experience—primarily psychological but philosophical and religious as well—of mankind. By no means does all that I have to say in this book fall into the category of certain knowledge. But I shall make every effort to alert the reader when I speak hypothetically.

Thus the knowledge we hope to obtain in what follows about the primordial existential mystery that is death will not be "scientific." But it will not for all of that be less authentically "human."

DEATH AND ITS MYSTERIES

I

All Men Are Mortal

*To myself I became a
great riddle.*
—ST. AUGUSTINE

❦

I HAVE borrowed the title of this chapter from one of Simone de Beauvoir's novels. I do not think that she intended her book to be anything like the final word on the subject of death. But she was very much concerned with exploring the rigorous law, both ontological and psychological, that all men must die. Raymond Fosca, the young and proud ruler of thirteenth century Carmona, was terrified of growing old and dying. The time of man on earth seemed to him too tragically short for realizing anything truly great for the glory of his city. He then met an old Jew who offered him an elixir of immortality. He had discovered it in Egypt but, despite his great fear of death, dared not drink, himself, so redoubtable did the perspective of a life without end strike him. Count Fosca, on the other hand, had no fear of not dying, especially since the elixir also guaranteed him perpetual youth. So he drank the elixir and became immune to death. For two centuries he governed his

3

city, waged wars, constructed new buildings, loved many
women and saw his children, grandchildren and great-grand-
children die. But lo and behold, he accomplished no more in
centuries than he could have in a reign of a few years. His
people lived as they pleased and refused to accept their leader's grandiose ideas. Instead of expressing admiration and
love, they feared him and wanted to be rid of him. Even his
own children thought and acted in terms of their short lives
and were not interested in the long-range projects of the
Count who could not die. After this painful revelation Fosca
left the city of Carmona and became the confidant and evil
demon to Emperor Charles V. Unable to realize his plan of
universal domination, which he had suggested to the Emperor, Fosca roamed the world. In the seventeenth century,
he participated in the discovery of Canada. In the eighteenth
century, he was active in the salon life of Paris. There, aris-
tocrats and beautiful ladies dreamed of progress and liberty
and thus prepared the climate, at once promising and horrifying, of the French Revolution. In 1789, Fosca took part
in that revolution, side by side with one of his great-grand-
children. He likewise fought in the revolutions of 1830 and
1848. Fosca was always on the side of the rebels because he
wanted the people to be happy, as he had in thirteenth-cen-
tury Carmona. He spent years in prison and in exile, and on
one occasion slept for sixty years. In the course of centuries
he loved, married and begot children. His wives and children
grew old and died, but he always remained the same. Gradually, he became terribly bored. He could no longer believe in
the future or in progress. The efforts of the most generous
of men appeared futile to him. Women at first believed that
they were exceptionally lucky to be loved by someone immortal, who would always remember them. But they were

soon undeceived and driven to madness when they realized that their immortal lover was incapable of giving himself, either in life or in death. In his eyes, all the deepest emotions were ephemeral. At bottom, and Fosca himself came to realize this, only those who must die are capable of truly loving life, undertaking great works, running risks and believing in the future. For such men the struggle for a better future, revolutions and scientific discoveries have meaning. It took Fosca centuries to understand this truth. He knew too many springtimes, too many roses, too many loves, to appreciate any of them. He was reduced to the playing out of a meaningless game. Only those who are mortal undertake long-range projects and act as if they were never going to die.

The implicit philosophical conclusion of Simone de Beauvoir's novel might be formulated in these words: It is good that man is mortal, for only on this condition can his existence be dramatic and intense. Those for whom life itself is the supreme good, no matter how it is lived, would not be likely to appreciate this thesis. They would undoubtedly envy Count Fosca and readily drink the elixir of immortality even though their eternity on earth would be as boring as his. But those who aspire to an authentic life will agree that Simone de Beauvoir's ideas at least merit consideration. We for our part agree with her contention that immortality would be a genuine good only if man were able to escape the earthly and temporal conditions and contingencies of his life.

[1] PHYSIOLOGICAL DEATH

We are not primarily concerned in this book with death as a physiological event. I will limit myself to recalling a few of its essential characteristics and refer the interested reader to an excellent little book on the subject by my friend Dr. Paul Chauchard, *La Mort, Que Sais-Je?*

The human organism is a complex of living cells. Each cell is mortal by nature, but new cells are born to replace dead ones in the body. After a given period of time, the renewal of living cells slows down and then ceases altogether. Biologically, natural death is not a sudden event but a slow process. From a biological point of view, we begin to age and die as soon as we are born. But the death of the individual takes place only after the last of the millions of cells that compose his body are dead. A cell dies when its protoplasmic activity ceases. Thus death is from this point of view the destruction of the cellular organization. But although the cells die and thereby bring about the death of the individual the atoms that make up the cells are not destroyed. They pass into other cells, other individuals, and it is in this sense that we can effectively speak of an essential kinship among all living creatures. The atoms that are today part of my corporeal makeup may one day be shared by animals and plants or perhaps other men. If we were willing to grant that atoms have souls, there would be a real sense in which we could speak of "metempsychosis."

The cell itself is a complex organism and as such cannot be considered immortal. Only protoplasm is. Neither science nor magic can prevent the death of cells and the organism composed of them; at most, their death can be delayed. It is not unlikely that the length of human life will one day be doubled or even tripled. But natural death has no final remedy. There can be no elixir of immortality.

Only death in old age can be called natural, and this only if it does not result from illness, as is frequently the case. Illness often proves mortal because the patient is already on the threshold of natural death and would probably have died soon anyway. The death of the young, whose cells are in a constant process of renewal, is always accidental. Hygiene and other measures can diminish the risk of accidental death and, thanks to these, the mortality rate among the young has appreciably declined in the past century. Bogomoletz and other biologists have attempted to rejuvenate the cells of old people and thus delay old age and death. Significant results have been obtained in this enterprise but can only extend as far as postponing death, not conquering it.

Species as well as individuals die. The only thing that escapes death in the empirical order is Life itself. And even that is endangered today by nuclear explosives.

Each individual has the right to want to follow Count Fosca's example and seek ways and means of avoiding the fatality of death. Since men are generally of the opinion that their species enjoys a particularly lofty dignity among living things, it is logical for them to try to save mankind from total extinction. But as soon as we view matters from the point of view of life in general we must recognize that death is necessary to make the emergence of new individuals and new species possible. Paul Chauchard says that "it would take less than two days for the progeny of a single bacterium to populate the face of the earth if they all survived; an infusorium would take forty-two days; a fly one year; a codfish four years, a rat eight years; a white clover eleven years, and the elephant more than a century." To obviate the absolute necessity of death, the reproduction of living things would have had to cease soon after it began. The consequence of this would be the absence of all growth, all evolution of the species. Man, the result of a long evolutionary process, would never have appeared on earth or, on the assumption that he was "created" on the first day of the biosphere, would never have evolved to his present state. In a word, we can conceive of the absence of death only in an entirely static universe where a determined number of members of different species would have been created in the beginning and remained constant for the duration. I do not know whether such a universe would have been preferable to our own. But there is no doubt that in an evolutionary universe death is a necessity. Understanding this is preliminary to study of or mediation on the mystery of death.

[2] THE EXPERIENCE OF DEATH

Strictly speaking, we can have no immediate experience of death, either our own or that of others. The loss of consciousness is one of the signs of individual death even though we do not die each time we lose consciousness. Even those who have experienced prolonged comas during which they seemed to be dead cannot tell us anything about the experience of death for the simple reason that they did not die. The Gospel speaks of Lazarus and two others Christ is reported to have raised from the dead. But none of them said anything about his death. Moreover, modern exegetes are inclined to think that neither the daughter of the centurion nor the son of the widow of Naim were dead in the clinical sense of the word, and that they underwent miraculous cures rather than resurrection. Lazarus, on the other hand, is thought to have been really dead, since he was three days in the tomb. But the evangelists tell us absolutely nothing about his experience of death. The same is true of the many accounts in Christian and other hagiographies according to which the dead were raised by the saints. Even legends, in which human imagination is given the greatest freedom, are extremely discreet about the experience of death.

Some authors think that the closest analogy to the experience of death is mystical ecstasy. St. Paul, Theresa of Avila and a number of other mystics have made this comparison. After being taken up into the "third heaven," Paul expressed the desire to die in order to recapture a similar happiness. But, instead of giving us a detailed account of his experience, Paul said that the language of man is incapable of describing the marvels he witnessed. We shall have occasion later to discuss the value of mediums and the authenticity of the "communications" the deceased are said to impart to them.

Karl Jung, as is well known, consecrated a considerable part of his work to the study of the mythologies of different races. He considered mythology to be a valuable source of information concerning the collective unconscious, which he supposed to be common to all men. He pointed out that in many mythologies death is compared to a return to the womb, where the dead are thought to be reborn. On this basis many authors postulate a parallel between death and birth. Like birth, death brings about a radical mutation in the condition of the living being. There is unquestionably much that is valuable in this image and we will examine it in more detail later on. But since we have no direct knowledge of our own birth, and since no one else does either, we must admit that the comparison between death and birth cannot tell us anything specific about the experience of death.

Our experience of death can only be indirect. It is in the presence of another's death that man normally becomes aware that all men are mortal and concludes that he too must die. According to Heidegger we are only capable of communicating our more banal experiences. The deep experiences of life are by nature incommunicable. Since death is one of those basic experiences the spectacle of another's death, no matter how close to us he may have been, would not constitute a genuine psychological experience. In seeing others die we become convinced of our own mortality but as long as we are alive it is merely "someone else" who dies, always another with whom we have no possibility of communicating in depth. My own experience, both direct and indirect, of interhuman relations prohibits my sharing Heidegger's pessimism concerning the radical incommunicability of basic experiences. But I admit that such communication is difficult. As a rule we can only communicate with those to whom we are bound by deep emotional bonds. The death of strangers is impersonal and tells us nothing essential about our own death. This perhaps explains the frightening indifference of individuals and peoples confronted with the death of others as a result of war, famine or other catastrophes. For the Germans contaminated by Hitler's racism, it was the impersonal "other" who died in the crematory ovens of Dachau. The Americans, however humanitarian and compassionate they may otherwise be, also looked upon the victims of Hiroshima impersonally. This is also true of the attitude of the majority of Frenchmen toward the atrocities committed in Algeria and other colonies but a short time ago. As I write these lines the news media carry reports of the mass murder of noncombatants in Vietnam by American soldiers convinced that they are serving the cause of freedom and democracy. We are also informed by the same media about the ravages of famine in India while the Western nations are concerned about over-eating. If the death of the Vietnamese and Indians scarcely disturbs most of us, and does not afford even an indirect experience of

death, it is again because as far as we are concerned it is the
anonymous "other" who dies.

But those close to us die too, those with whom our communication is not limited to banalities but touches upon the
essential. Their death constitutes an authentic experience of
death for us; a part of us dies with them. This is illustrated
by a famous passage in St. Augustine's *Confessions* where
he speaks of the death of his closest friend:

"During those years, when I first began to teach—it was
in the town in which I was born—I gained a friend, my equal
in age, flowering like me with youth, and very dear to me
because of a community of interests. As a boy, he had grown
up with me, we had gone to school together, and had played
games together. . . . This man was now wandering with me in
spirit, and my soul could not endure to be without him. But
behold, you were close at the back of those fleeing from you,
you who are at once the God of vengeance and the fount
of mercy, who in a marvellous manner convert us to yourself. Behold, you took the man from this life when he had
scarce completed a year in my friendship, sweet to me above
every sweetness of that life of mine. . . .

"Tormented by fever, he lay for a long time senseless in a
deadly sweat, and when his life was despaired of, he was bap-
tized while unconscious. . . . After a few days, while I was
absent, he was attacked again by the fever and died.

"My heart was made dark by sorrow, and whatever I looked
upon was death. My native place was a torment to me, and
my father's house was a strange unhappiness. Whatsoever I
had done together with him was, apart from him, turned into
cruel torture. My eyes sought for him on every side, and he
was not given to them. I hated all things, because they no

longer held him. Nor could they now say to me, 'Here he comes,' as they did in his absence from them when he lived. To myself I became a great riddle, and I questioned my soul as to why it was sad and why it afflicted me so grievously, and it could answer me nothing. If I said to it, 'Hope in God,' it did right not to obey me, for the man, that most dear one whom she had lost, was more real and more good to her than the fantasy in which she was bade to hope. Only weeping was sweet to me, and it was my friend's successor in my soul's delights. . . .

"I marvelled that other men should live, because he, whom I had loved as if he would never die, was dead. I marveled more that I, his second self, could live when he was dead. Well has someone said of his friend that he is half his soul. For I thought that my soul and his soul were but one soul in two bodies. Therefore, my life was a horror to me, because I would not live as but a half. Perhaps because of this I feared to die, lest he whom I had loved so much should wholly die."

There is no doubt that St. Augustine had a real experience of death in the death of his friend. By identifying with him, he experienced, as it were, his own death. He also proved himself extremely capable of the kind of communication that Heidegger says is impossible. Similar testimonies can be found in the works of such writers as Goethe, Montaigne and others who knew the painful experience of death through the loss of a dear friend. Perhaps someday, when human solidarity and our capacity to love all men as we love ourselves are more highly developed, we will not be so indifferent to the death of black people in Africa or yellow people in Asia; perhaps then the wars and famines that victimize them will affect us as the death of Augustine's friend affected him.

The German philosopher, Max Scheler, says that every human being possesses in one form or another an intuitive certainty of his own death. Psychologists and philosophers have tried to show that some of the higher forms of animal life also have some knowledge of their impending death. They note the case of cats and dogs who hide themselves in order to die privately; other animals flee when death is imminent. There is a case on record of a mortally wounded dog affectionately licking his master's hand in a farewell gesture. It is also said that cattle and other domestic animals in slaughterhouses, having presentiments of their death, emit cries of distress and try to save themselves.

I obviously do not accept the Cartesian theory which holds that animals are mere machines and have no real psychic life. Today no psychologist or philosopher would doubt the existence of psychic activity in animals. In fact that activity is highly developed in some of the higher forms of animal life. But we should avoid the opposite error of interpreting animal behavior in terms of what we know about human psychology. The psychic life of animals constitutes a vast domain that deserves study in its own right. When this autonomy is observed, we discover that the so-called presentiment of death in animals is nothing of the sort, that the behavior involved must be interpreted in other terms. Specialists in animal psychology are agreed that even the most psychically developed animals are only aware of the present, that a sense of the future and the possible is completely lacking in them. They have no abstractive ability at all. An animal is instinctively aware of an immediate danger but it cannot conclude from the death of another animal that death is common to the species as such. In reality the animal is only species; to claim awareness of the individual for him is an anthropomorphic projection.

Those who compare animal death to human death have an anthropomorphic vision of animals and an animalistic vision of man. Animals, it is true, show signs of distress somewhat similar to human mourning in the presence of the death of other members of their species. But they are still unaware of their own deaths or death in general. And there is no evidence that even such highly psychic animals as monkeys and elephants bury their dead. Death is neither a problem nor a mystery for animals.

Of all the living species in our universe, only man knows that he is mortal. It seems that self-consciousness emerged almost simultaneously with his consciousness of death. Nor do we have any evidence that he has ever considered death to be a banal event. Only in our time, and in the materially prosperous West, do men see death as a simple biological fact. But it should be noted that they usually consider the death of others in this perspective rather than their own. I know many materialists who are much concerned with dying and being buried in proper style.

It is well known that paleontologists can determine that the remains of centuries ago are human on the basis of evidence furnished by funeral rites and honors rendered to the deceased. From the earliest beginnings of time man has been characterized by a minimal sense of individuality, by a certain capacity to project into the future, from the actual to the possible, and to infer his own fate from the fate of others. In this sense we can say that only man's death is an actual going away, a departure. And it leaves a profound impression upon those who survive.

Thus the death of another can be a genuine experience of death for us on condition that we experience it deeply, that is to say, identify to some extent with the other's death. We have already noted that those in whom the universal sense of human solidarity is highly developed experience each death as a harbinger of their own death, indeed *as* their own death. But ordinarily men can achieve this experience only when loved ones die.

Cathy, an aware and intelligent girl of four, knows that her two grandparents are dead. But she refers to this fact without any emotion, apparently without any precise idea of its meaning. She had scarcely known them and they died far from her home. Her reaction to their death is probably somewhat as though she had been told that they live in a foreign country or have taken a trip. Cathy had a domesticated sparrow of which she was very fond. One day while playing she accidentally fell on the bird and killed it. She was heartbroken. When her mother told her that the bird was dead she grew pensive. Only then did she begin to understand the meaning of her grandparents' death. They no longer move, they cannot talk, they are cold. They were disposed of as her pet was disposed of. In the following days she constantly asked such questions as, "Will my nurse die soon? Will mother and father also die? Must all men die?" Finally, she asked, "Will Cathy die too?" It was her first affective experience of death which quite normally led to an awareness of her own mortality and the notion of death in general. I had the opportunity to talk with Cathy about this experience some fourteen years after it happened. She remembers it vividly although she has almost completely forgotten other things that happened in her life at that time. If a psychoanalyst were one day to explore her unconscious I have no doubt that he would discover that the accidental death of her pet had left a profound impression on the little girl.

My personal experience of death came early in life. As a

child I lived in the country and frequently went hunting with my grandfather. But the deaths of animals didn't seem to have any particular effect on me. Then one day my dog died as a result of a gunshot wound and the tragedy of the event impressed me deeply. When we learned that my father had been killed in the war, my brother, who was then four years old, was quite undisturbed. But I reacted very differently, although I was only three years older. My imagination immediately related my father's death to that of my dog.

The child's emotional experience of death and awareness of his own mortal condition generally proves to be very important for his general psychic maturity. In the course of my psychotherapeutic practice I have frequently observed that those who have been dramatically and brutally introduced to death have a pessimistic attitude toward life and are frequently disturbed, although they are unaware of the connection between their neuroses and their experiences of death. However, we must not conclude hastily that all neurotics and pessimists have had similar experiences. There are many causes of such conditions. On the other hand, those whose childhood experiences of death were less traumatic are more inclined to see it as a natural event, a delivery from sickness and suffering. It goes without saying that the religious doctrine of immortality greatly helps the child to see death as a natural event rather than an irremediable catastrophe.

In view of the foregoing we might raise this question: Should children be allowed to witness the last agony and death of their grandparents or other close relatives? There doesn't seem to me to be any one answer to this question. I don't think it is advisable for children to be in the presence of great suffering. On the other hand, where the pain is slight and the last moments of the dying person are marked by great spiritual serenity the experience can only be beneficial to the child and enable him to better understand death as the fulfillment of life. In any event, the child ought to be prepared for his encounter with the redoubtable and mysterious reality of death. Furthermore, a great deal depends on the behavior of adults. The child should never learn of a loved one's death suddenly in an atmosphere of weeping and distress, but should be told as calmly as possible.

Accidental deaths are especially traumatic. One of my patients, twenty-two years old, came to me in an acute nervous condition. Nightmares awakened him at night; he suffered from heart palpitation and was in a constant cold sweat. Although he was physically healthy, there were days when he dared not leave the house for fear of falling down in the street. I learned that when he was a mere three-year-old he had been in an automobile accident that took the life of his mother and seriously injured several others, although he himself escaped with minor injuries. Consciously he did not remember the accident, but subconsciously he was profoundly disturbed by this shocking encounter with death. After therapy he understood why his nightmares always centered on accidents and catastrophes. We might note in passing that a sudden experience of death can be harmful for adults as well as children.

[3]   THE DEATH INSTINCT

Those who are not familiar with psychoanalytic literature will no doubt be surprised by the title of this section. For it is commonly thought that all of our instincts—for food, sex and safety—are life instincts. Moreover, Freud himself long held the libido to be the common energy of all the instincts and called it the life instinct. But the founder of psycho-analysis gradually elaborated the concept of a death instinct which he contrasted with the libido and finally considered more fundamental than the life instincts.

Freud defined instinct as the expression of a drive inherent in every living organism. Its principal function was to re-establish an anterior state which the organism was forced to renounce as the result of external disturbing pressures. This definition by no means meets with the common agreement of all biologists. But what is important for our purposes here is to understand how Freud constructed his theory of the death instinct.

As a good clinician, Freud paid attention to his patients' reactions, both conscious and unconscious, to death. He observed that some people have attitudes toward life that are clearly negative. There are victims of anorexia, who refuse to eat. It is indicative that they often dream of their own deaths as well as those of people close to them, and as happy events rather than as something sad. Normally their behavior will lead to death if they cannot be fed in spite of themselves. Others endeavor to destroy themselves by abusing alcohol or other intoxicants. Generalizing, as was his tendency, Freud went on to consider all dangerous behavior as manifestations of the death instinct. Those who engage in mountain climb-ing, deep-sea diving and the exploration of deserts and virgin forests were in his mind all unconsciously seeking an escape from life in death. In a word, anything in the nature of dan-ger, a serious risk or an exceptional effort was for Freud and his followers an instance of aggression against oneself and a manifestation of the will to die. All forms of heroism were suspect because they dissimulate a death wish. All such activi-ties as voluntary defense of one's country, attempts to save a drowning person or caring for the seriously ill are alike the signs of an unconscious desire to die. According to this logic only the perfectly egotistical and narcissistic person would escape the contamination of the death wish. Generosity, courage and altruism would be merely guises of masochism, and all forms of masochism would be in the service of death. The same would be true of sadistic behavior. Freud always considered sadism and maschoism as two faces of the same destructive tendency.

The desire to destroy oneself or another come to the same thing in the final analysis. Both are expressions of the same hostility toward life. Freud's knowledge of the human soul and what he observed in the world about him reinforced his constitutional pessimism. In history as well as in human relations, he saw primarily hatred and cruelty. Wars, religious and racial persecution and the many crimes of man were for him the very stuff of the human condition. Man's exploitation of man, authoritarianism, contempt and deceit were more attentuated expressions of the same sadism and were equally manifestions of the death wish.

There can be no questioning of the facts Freud observed. But he was no mere clinician. He drew doctrinal conclusions from the material furnished by his patients and erected them into a rigid system. Seeing everywhere the work of forces hostile to life and man's impulse to destroy himself, while at the same time faithful to his materialistic-mechanist concept of the human psyche, Freud was altogether consistent in postulating the death instinct. At first he considered it equal to the life instinct. He divided all instincts into two principal classes: the one serving Eros, the other Thanatos. But as he grew older, experienced more intimately the infirmities of man and helplessly witnessed the Nazi persecution of the Jewish people, with whom he had always felt a deep solidarity, Freud's pessimism deepened. He finally came to view the death wish as man's first and essential instinct, all others being either subordinate to or vanquished by it. Here, in summary form, is the intellectual rationalization of Freud's psychological pessimism:

As was said earlier, the purpose of every instinct is to conserve a naturally given order or to restore it if it has been disturbed. Now Freud reasoned that the inorganic and nonliving are anterior to the organic and living. Thus the emergence of life, especially conscious life, must be seen as a disturbance, an imbalance, somehow introduced into the kingdom of death from without. It would therefore be normal, indeed necessary, for there to have been an instinct before the life instinct. Following the universal law of entropy, life would normally tend to revert to its original inorganic state. The so-called instincts of life and preservation can only superficially be considered life-serving. When regarded more closely they are merely guises for the death instinct. For thinkers like Teilhard de Chardin and the dialectical materialists, the evolution from matter to life is of the qualitative order and excludes a return to some primitive state. Freud's conception, on the other hand, is aligned with the old materialist-mechanist theory. Consequently, he sees only a simple quantitative process which adds nothing really new to the static order of matter.

It is worth while pointing out that Sartre's theory of being as an opaque and incomprehensible "in itself" and human reality as a "for itself" that is, to be sure, translucent but fragile and without justification, resembles in more ways than one Freud's concept of life and death—although it is better elaborated philosophically than the latter. Both have a radically pessimistic view of life and of the future. Sartre is just as materialistic as Freud and, in spite of his dialectical pretensions, his materialism is just as mechanistic (which is to say pre-Marxist) as the Viennese master's. Sartre also thinks that life and spirit are more or less fortuitous products of the blind forces of the inorganic universe rather than conquests of evolution. Thus Marxists are understandably contemptuous of both Sartre and Freud, although Sartre often poses as a faithful fellow traveller. Both thinkers are at opposite poles from the evolutionary concepts represented by Teilhard de Chardin. According to Teilhard, life evolved from matter, and the spirit from animal life. An authentic continuity obtains between the hylosphere, the biosphere and the noosphere. But the new phase of the universe in a constant state of becoming is not an accidental disorder introduced into a prior state but the normal realization of the depositing of energy. It follows that life does not regress toward the inorganic but tends toward the creation of increasingly more perfect and complex forms of life. That is why Marxist thinkers are intellectually more akin to Teilhard de Chardin than either Sartre or Freud. That is why, too, both the disciples of Teilhard and the Marxists are enthusiastic about Teilhard's concept of evolution, which exalts life and predicts its final triumph.

It is important to emphasize the fact that Freud's theory of the death wish is not based on his scientific experience. It originates in his pessimism and personal disappointments. This would seem to explain why many of his most faithful disciples make no reference to this doctrine and do not even seem to consider it a tenable hypothesis. I have the greatest admiration for Freud's genius and, like all who are engaged in depth psychology, am greatly indebted to him. It goes without saying that I have great compassion for the terrible suffering of both body and soul he endured in the course of his long lifetime. Thus I understand only too well the psychological mechanisms that led Freud to postulate the existence of a death wish and accord it a preponderant place in his system. But understanding and compassion for the man do not oblige me to accept his philosophy. The tragedy of Freud is that the majority of his disciples, in this as other matters, were inclined to interpret observable reality in terms of his theory rather than to subject the latter to thoroughgoing criticism. This lack of intellectual courage on the part of many of his followers has made of Freudianism a kind of new scholasticism. Freud was imbued with nineteenth-century scientism and inclined to confer dogmatic value upon even his most hazardous hypotheses.

When life and the data of consciousness are observed without doctrinal prejudice, there is no clear evidence of a death wish. In animals and in man all instincts are in the service of life. This is true of the nutritional and sexual instincts as well as the instinct of aggression, which inspired the theory under criticism here. We readily agree with Freud that many people give proof of a surprising eagerness to sow the seeds of death, to destroy themselves as well as others. Men like Hitler and Stalin behaved as though killing were the only value, as though life were an evil that had to be extirpated at all costs. The most reliable information indicates that fifteen million Soviet citizens died under Stalin. Hitler victimized many more, although for the most part not members of his own race. Both dictators succeeded in molding innumerable brave Russians and Germans into fanatical agents of death, men who today are unable to understand the sadistic pleasure they took in being more cruel than strict obedience to orders demanded. Must we say that these executioners were impelled by a strong

death instinct? I do not think so. In fact both Hitler and
Stalin were convinced that they were the artisans of a better
future for their peoples. I would say that their deeds and the
sadistic actions of those under their orders were due rather
to the atrophy of the life instinct. The causes of such atrophy
are to be found in unconscious emotional conflicts. I have
shown elsewhere (See my *The Psychology of Love*) that sexual perversions, far from being the result of a "normal"
impulse of the sexual instinct, are the consequence of its
atrophy. I would say the same of the so-called death wish.

Suppose a child refuses to eat and must be forced to take
nourishment? Does this mean that a death instinct is operative? Not necessarily. It seems more plausible to say that the
child's life instinct has been inhibited by premature weaning.
A failure in instinctive behavior does not constitute evidence
in favor of the opposite instinct.

Consider a case of adult anorexia. Luke, a twenty-three-
year-old student, was sent to me by his doctor. For two years
he had been unable to swallow liquid. Medical treatment had
proved ineffective. To prevent complete dehydration a special
gruel, which he could swallow with difficulty, was prescribed.
He was pronounced physically sound, but his normal reflexes
of swallowing did not function. More seriously, the young
man had for the past three days been unable to take any
solids. This well-built and intelligent young man was visibly
wasting away. His parents were not unreasonably concerned.
Could it be said that a subconscious death instinct was responsible for his trouble even though consciously he was intensely
fond of life? An orthodox Freudian would probably diagnose
his case in this manner. But I refused to take that approach.
There was an immediate rapport between Luke and myself.
That evening he was able to swallow some food. It became

clear in the course of treatment that anxiety, originating in serious emotional conflicts with his mother which he had suppressed, was the cause of the paralysis of his life instinct. At the rate of several sessions a week we succeeded in progressively dislodging the "knot" that was literally strangling him. Luke took a renewed interest in life, his aggressiveness toward his parents diminished, he gradually became capable of eating normally and, toward the end of his treatment, even succeeded in drinking. From the beginning I was quite sure that the atrophy in this case was emotional in origin and this conviction dictated my therapeutic approach. Of course the results might not have been so quick with another patient. In that case artificial nourishment would have been necessary. We were lucky.

I have had the opportunity to observe and analyze many masochists and sadists. I have never found even one instance of a death instinct in them and no doctrinal prejudices would have prevented my admitting this cause of destructiveness toward self or others were there any evidence for it. What the masochist actually seeks is not self-destruction bu the perverse pleasure that suffering and humiliation procure him. I have already suggested an explanation for the behavior of such monstrous sadists as Hitler and Stalin. They tortured and killed out of the conviction that they were acting for the welfare of their peoples. Similarly, the ordinary sadist or masochist is not motivated for reasons of destruction as such but for pleasure. In both cases a desire for pleasure masks a life instinct that has been disturbed or perverted by subconscious psychic conflicts.

Metchnikoff and several other biologists and psychoanalysts hold that the death instinct is obvious in old people, that they clearly desire death as a return to a supposed primitive state of inertia and the inorganic. Here again, theory deforms the psychological reality. It is a common observation that the life instincts of many old people are markedly reactivated as they approach the threshold of death. Although ill and aware that they are near death, they cling to life and beg the doctor to prolong it as long as possible even though their last days will be marked by great suffering. They often hope to be cured even when rationally they know full well that there is no possibility of this. The fact that they eventually resign themselves to the inevitable is due more to the weakened condition of the life instinct than to the triumph of the death instinct. In the case of believers the life instinct of those near death is transmitted into a desire for eternal life. We might legitimately presume that the frequent conversions of agnostics and atheists on their deathbeds can be at least partially explained as a last resurgence of the life instinct. As we shall see later, the death instinct is not even evident in those who commit suicide.

[4]   THE SCANDAL OF DEATH

It is difficult to envisage our death as a *natural* phenomenon. When we speak of death in general or the death of strangers we consider it perfectly natural and compare it poetically to the autumnal fall of leaves. We readily agree that death in general is absolutely necessary in a universe that is as yet in a state of unfulfillment. But we see our own death or the death of anyone close to us as a threat, indeed a scandalous injustice. I once consoled a young girl whose grandmother had died by saying that her death was in the normal order of things since she was over eighty years old. That was easy enough for me. But the young girl, who had been raised by her grandmother and was deeply attached to her, could not accept such reasoning. She saw in this death an injustice and blasphemed against God, in whom she believed, accusing him of being her grandmother's assassin. Such extreme reactions are rare. Still we seldom hear anyone say of a beloved one's death, "It was normal and according to the order of things." We at least feel that the person's death could have been postponed.

It was stated earlier that no man can have a direct experience of his own death. We conclude that all living things, including ourselves, are mortal because we are familiar with the death of others and know that we are like them. This indirect character of our experience of death combined with a strong life instinct undoubtedly explains why most men, while admitting rationally that they are mortal, have great difficulty in believing in their own death or those of dear ones. As Goethe wrote to Eckermann: "Death is something so strange that in spite of our experience of it we do not think it is possible for those we cherish; it always surprises us as something unbelievable and paradoxical." Even when we know well in advance that someone close to us is mortally ill, his death always comes to us as something "unbelievable and paradoxical." I recall the despairing rebellion of a young man afflicted with tuberculosis who realized that he had not long to live. The hospital chaplain exhorted him to accept the inevitable and marshalled a multitude of arguments to show that death was natural. But to no avail. The young man wanted to live and thought it scandalous to die after having lived such a short time. Even promises of eternal life could not console him. As we shall see later, death ceases to be an intolerable scandal only when we know that we are dying for something.

According to the almost unanimous testimony of the ethnologists, primitive peoples rarely consider death the natural end of life. It is generally attributed to more-or-less fortuitous causes—the machinations of sorcerers, the ingratitude of a son, or malevolent spirits. The Bible, reporting an undoubtedly ancient Semitic belief and one that is not without parallel in other traditions, considers the death of the individual and death in general as a punishment inflicted by God for the sin of disobedience committed by the first human couple. In this perspective, death is no longer an accident but a necessity. For centuries Christian theologians interpreted the Biblical narrative literally and viewed death as a violation of the natural order. Only gradually did they come to think of death as the normal end of human life. This attitude is confirmed by the example of Christ who did not abolish death even though he triumphed over the reign of sin. Thus modern theologians attribute only the painful, harrowing aspect of death to Adam's sin. Without sin, they say, the passage from time to eternity would be effected without anxiety and suffering.

In the middle ages the Christian people expected death to re-establish the order of justice violated by the wicked. The Christian conscience had progressed to a point where it could no longer admit that a world in which the just suffered and the wicked triumphed was normal or willed by God. Perhaps somewhat simplistically, they generally identified the wicked with the rich and powerful and the just with the poor and weak. With few exceptions (such as peasant uprisings and other gestures of rebellion) they entertained little hope of establishing the order of justice in this world. But inspired by the evangelical parables of Lazarus and others, the people firmly believed that justice would be restored after death. The macabre dances represented in sculpture and paintings in almost all the medieval churches energetically proclaim that death will make no distinction between the great and the small, the rich and the poor. They represent popes, emperors, lords and serfs before the same judge. Each is shown as he will be for all eternity. Death ignores class and caste; it only respects what man is in himself, in his inmost heart. And it was principally the crowned and mitred heads that medieval artists numbered among the damned.

It took many centuries for men, at least in the West, to understand death in the perspective of personal destiny. A long process of individualization was necessary for this. In the nineteenth century many psychologists and sociologists held that "in the beginning" men lived in nomadic tribes and had only a collective consciousness. Freud in particular made extended and abusive use of this hypothesis. According to him it was an Oedipal crime which first struck the spark of individual consciousness in the group. The legend invented by Freud is borne out by certain psychological facts but there is no historical proof to support it. The available evidence indicates that man has always been conscious of himself as an individual. But it is true that individual consciousness was very weak in primitive peoples where clan or tribal consciousness prevailed. Death was looked upon more as the loss of a member of the clan than an individual loss. Sometimes it was believed that restitution could be made for the loss by giving the deceased's name and function to another member of the group. It is very probable that the deep religious meaning of cannibalism is to be found in this same desire to conserve for the clan the virtues and energies possessed by the deceased.

Rudimentary at first, individual consciousness gradually became more pronounced. Not only did each individual recognize himself as distinct from others but he also claimed a personal dignity that owed nothing to his place in a given

social group. And, by analogy, the same personal dignity was
recognized in all others. Thus death ceased to be a mere collective fact and henceforth signified the supreme scandal of
each individual's personal history. It marked the end of all
his potential, of any further chance. At first only members
of the same tribe or city were thought to possess this personal
quality. As a result they were deemed worthy of protection
and respect. Others were strangers and barbarians, enemies.
Their death had no importance and there was no crime in
killing them for any reason judged "good."

Even today, when individual consciousness has evolved to
the point where we can speak of "the eminent dignity of the
human person," most of us do not react in the same way to
the death of all men. Many people are scarcely touched by
newspaper reports of those who have perished by famine or
natural catastrophes in distant lands. Some even look upon
such events as nature's way of controlling the population
explosion. Examples abound to demonstrate that we are all
to some extent "primitives" in our attitude toward the death
of others. We have only to think of Algeria or the Nazi concentration camps. There is also the case of the American
Negro, whose summary and often massive executions at the
hands of the Ku Klux Klan or other racists barely arouse the
white majority's indignation, while a crime committed against
a white man by a Negro provokes the greatest outrage.

Nonetheless, these facts are less indicative of a *state* of
contemporary consciousness than a more-or-less lasting crisis
of that consciousness, which can be described as inhibited or
temporarily atrophied by the collective neurosis. In general,
the death of any individual takes on the character of an important event in modern civilized societies. True, we might
contest the usefulness of prolonging the life of a hopelessly

ill old person by artificial means. We might find the efforts made in Africa and Asia to diminish the infant mortality rate illogical when it is difficult if not impossible to nourish the present population. But these efforts are nonetheless homage rendered to life. It is a noble thing to combat death, to do what we can to prevent it from stamping the destiny of a man with a definitive seal.

Whatever the success of our efforts against death, we all know that it is inevitable, that none can escape it, that it is a sociological as well as a biological necessity. Let us end this chapter with a final question: when and how should we die? The philosopher Louis Lavelle, whose work is characterized by a concern for inwardness, writes: "Delicate natures desire a slow death for which they may prepare at length and in which life progressively diminishes." Men of action generally prefer a sudden death in the full flush of their powers. Life would be uninteresting for them if illness and old age prevented their living intensely. But it is not unusual to see those who desired a sudden death when they were young and healthy cling tenaciously to life when they are old and sick. Moreover, with the exception of suicide cases, which we will analyze later, no one chooses the time or the manner of his death. It would be enough if we could accept it serenely and without fear when it comes.

II

The Fear of Death

It is not death I fear
but dying.
— MONTAIGNE

W E must clearly distinguish between fear of death and
anxiety about death. A certain instinctive fear of death is a
perfectly normal reaction. This is all the more true since we
hold, in opposition to Freud, that only life instincts exist.
Anything that conflicts with an instinct, especially one so
fundamental as the life instinct, necessarily appears as aggression, and nothing is more normal than to fear aggression. On
the other hand, if we admitted the existence of a death instinct,
especially of one more basic than the life instinct, the fear of
death would be a more-or-less serious pathological anomaly.
But in our view, fear of death is neither a weakness nor an evil
to be eradicated, but a *virtue* which generally renders precious
services to life. In its absence, the search for pleasure would
probably lead to mortal catastrophe. Furthermore, children,
who know no fear and certainly not of death, must be taught
caution if they are not to harm themselves. It may be said

31

that fear of death exercises a quite positive function, not only because it protects us against death, but also because it stimulates us and increases our joy in living. We saw in the first chapter, in the example of Count Fosca, how boring and lacking in joy the life of one who has no fear of death can be.

But anxiety about death is a different matter. According to Spinoza it is one of the fundamental states of human sensibility; it transports us outside of ourselves into a reality that denies our existence. It expresses nothing positive since it is a negation and not a transcendence of existence. On the contrary, anxious fear of death paralyzes action, renders man unsuited for life and sometimes even deprives him of the desire to live. Fear, as we have seen, serves life; but anxiety serves death. Thus a relatively large number of those who commit suicide choose voluntary death because they are overcome by the anxiety which the thought of death inspires in them. All psychologists know that anxiety, far from preserving us from an apprehended danger, precipitates us toward it. A fortune teller had predicted that a young girl would kill her husband on February Fourteenth. For several years the girl lived in fear and trembling during the weeks preceding that fatal date. Two or three days before the Fourteenth, she would find some excuse to absent herself from her home and husband. About five years later she broke down. Her anxiety had become so intense that the only way she could find release was to kill her sleeping husband with an axe. The jury and public opinion had great difficulty in understanding this homicide. The couple had been on good terms, and even though the woman was nervous and highly emotional she was not mad. An expert psychiatrist pointed out the determining role of anxiety in this case. In the name of justice the jury should not have condemned the young woman but the fortune teller, who was dangerously ignorant of the psychological mechanisms her trade could set in action.

[I]   THE FEAR OF DEATH AMONG "PRIMITIVE" PEOPLES

Funeral rites occupy a place of great importance in the social life of all "primitive" peoples. We noted earlier that evidence of such rites and ceremonies most often permit us to conclude that the prehistoric inhabitants of such-and-such a place were human. In our civilized societies, the varied pomp associated with funerals is intended to honor the deceased and give evidence that he lives on in our memory. This does not seem to have been the case with primitive peoples. Ethnologists agree that, for them, the principal cause of rites and ceremonies is fear of the deceased person himself.

Thus primitives fear death less than the dead. Even a close relative is not supposed to have a friendly attitude toward the deceased. On the contrary, the latter is believed to be evil and hostile, seeking to harm the living. He is believed to be present in savage beasts, destructive storms and lightning. The malevolence of the deceased must be neutralized and this is one of the principal reasons for different magical techniques. Tears and lamentations are intended to prove to the deceased how much his absence is regretted. Whether they be sincere or simulated, their principal aim is to exorcise fear. Incantatory rites practiced at funerals are designed to ward off the anger of the deceased. In Malaysia there is a tribe whose fear of a departed member of the family is so great that they dare not bury him for fear of being sullied by the physical contact. His body is abandoned and the family remove themselves as far as possible in the hope of not being found.

But this elementary and irrational terror of death and the

dead is not characteristic of "primitives alone." The literature of all civilized peoples abounds with accounts of ghosts and haunted houses. Such spirits have the power to trouble the sleep of even convinced materialists. The story is told that in a city of Touraine a large, beautiful house stood empty for many years. No one would buy or rent it because it was believed to be haunted by a young woman who had committed suicide there many years ago after a disappointment in love. One day a stranger in the city, ignorant of these stories, bought it, but the ghost is said to have raised such an uproar each night that he could not sleep in peace. Then a brave soul, who believed in nothing supernatural, let alone ghost stories, came forth and bet that he could spend the night in the haunted house. The next morning, he was found hanged. Those who told me this story do not believe in any form of survival after death; but they admit that they are troubled by such phenomena.

The fear most people experience when passing through or near a cemetery at night is not greatly different from the primitive fear of death. Some years ago a group of young people who had been drinking too much decided to spend the night in a cemetery. They stole past the guard and took up positions at some distance from one another. Toward the middle of the night one of them became so terrified that his cries brought the police. He was taken to a hospital and had to undergo lengthy psychiatric treatment. Another was found dead of a heart attack. It may be supposed that in the nocturnal silence the young men saw ghosts—more likely rising from their own unconsciouses than from the graves. The "primitive" mentality survives in the psyches of even the most educated and rational men. It is buried more deeply in the unconscious and only emerges in special circumstances. Whatever explanations are offered, the fear of death and the dead seems to be rooted in the collective unconscious of the human race.

[2] IMAGINARY ANTICIPATION OF DEATH

A distinction is to be drawn between fear of the dead and fear of death. The first predominates among primitive peoples and is occasionally manifested among civilized peoples. But the second is much more common among civilized peoples. The fear of death which saddens the lives of so many men is closely related to their individuality. The more a man is conscious of himself as an individual rather than a member of a group, the greater is his fear of death. The cause of his fear is most often an imaginary anticipation of his own death.

It seems that most men imaginatively adopt a double perspective: They see themselves dying and dead as though they were outside of themselves, as though they were dead and yet living. They visualize the chagrin of their loved ones and the joy of their enemies. They often experience a horror of being buried in a common plot rather than in a private sepulchre. Whence those clauses in wills whereby men lay down minute instructions for their burials, often putting their heirs to no end of trouble.

One of my patients had read the frightening tales of Edgar Allan Poe in her youth. She was stimulated to imagine her own death and burials. She *saw* herself in her final suffering, then in the casket and finally buried in the humid and forlorn earth. She *saw* the grief of her loved ones. Sometimes matters were complicated by the memory of another Poe story, and she imagined that she was buried alive. She had a certain amount of money and, in her poor psychic health, she suspected her heirs of wanting to profit by one of her fainting spells to bury her alive. In many individuals I have interviewed, the fear of death expresses itself in a fear of being buried alive. There are many books with stories and anecdotes of apparent death, relating in imaginative detail its many variations. In discussion, those who have a morbid fear of being buried alive admit that the chances of this actually happening are slim. But their fear persists, which indicates that they are victims of the kind of imaginative projection we have just described.

An almost amusing case in point was an old doctor, a free-mason and notorious atheist. He knew that he was dying. His wife begged him to receive the last sacraments. He consented with this warning: "I warn you that if I find out all of this is a lie and if there is, as I believe, nothing beyond death, then, woman, you had better watch out!"

Even the most balanced of men finds it hard to keep calm when he thinks about his own death and imagines the cadaver he will be. The neurotic and superstitious are not alone in manifesting an interest in their future burial. John, sixty years old, well educated and a fervent Christian, confided to me that until he was fifty he had never worried about how he would die or where he would be buried. He was an avid swimmer and could envisage with the greatest serenity the possibility that he might drown and his body be consumed by fish. Or, if he died normally, he wanted to will his body to a medical school for dissection in the interests of scientific progress. He also regretted his Church's prohibition of crema-tion since he was an admirer of the Hindu custom of dispers-ing the ashes of the deceased on the water. In the past five years John has become more keenly aware of his age and no longer talks about his death so lightly. Not that he is afraid of death as such. His faith stands him in good stead in this respect. Nor is he afraid of being buried alive. But he is afraid of dying. He has seen men endure great suffering in their last moments and fears that, in such circumstances, his courage would fail him and he would set an example quite unbecoming a man of his faith. But he is primarily worried about his future burial. He is horrified at the prospect of being buried in a public cemetery or in one of those mausoleums where caskets are piled on top of each other. He wants to be buried in a village churchyard, preferably on a rise that affords a good view, and to have a beautiful cactus planted on his grave. He speaks of all this in ironic tones, as though mocking himself and others, but it is evident that in doing so he is trying to conceal the seriousness of his real preoccupation. He is aware that none of this will make any difference after he is dead. It is such concerns that motivate the instructions found in so many last testaments. From this point of view it does not seem that men have changed much since those distant times when the worst punishment that could be inflicted on an individual was deprivation of burial in his own city. We see in such attitudes one of the more common expressions of the fear of dying.

Many men would agree with Montaigne that it is not death they fear but dying. They are apprehensive about the often long and painful illness and the throes of agony that precede death. Today this fear centers primarily on cancer, which haunts the thoughts of many healthy people. Generally speaking, we envy old people who enjoy good health until the end and die in their sleep. Only this kind of death seems to be perfectly natural, the only kind that is not fearsome. A sudden death by accident should logically be just as desirable, since it too spares the suffering that accompanies a slow death. Yet most men fear a sudden death. This fear is logical for those who believe in an afterlife and a last judgment since a sudden death might deprive them of an opportunity to prepare to meet the supreme judge. Catholics pray to be spared "a sudden and unexpected death." This fear is more illogical among unbelievers; yet it exists, which seems to prove that under the façade of rational convictions the unconscious is more-or-less the same in all men. Nearly everyone considers a sudden or premature death to be a violation of the pre-established order of things, whether or not he intellectually admits the existence of such an order.

If human existence obeyed the laws of rational logic, it would seem that those who live most intensely and love life most passionately would most fear death. For wouldn't death terminate something very precious to them? On the other hand, the tired and discouraged, all those who find life a painful burden should welcome it as a deliverance from their miseries. But experience shows this not to be the case.

During the last war I had frequent occasion to note that those who vegetate more than they live were the most afraid and the first to run for the shelters during air raids. Panic was almost always greatest in hospitals for incurable cases and homes for old people. In 1944 when the city where I lived was bombed frequently, I had in my employ a house servant whose life was as miserable as could be imagined. Her drunkard husband beat her, she rarely had enough to eat and her body was racked by a terminal disease. As soon as the sirens sounded she dropped whatever she was doing and fled to the nearest shelter, despite the fact that she was forbidden to run by her doctor. I tried to persuade her that for a good Christian the moment of death was not that important and that in any case her life was not very joyful. She replied that it was something stronger than she was. The thought of death terrified her, especially the thought of a violent death.

On the other hand, I observed that those whose lives were full and exciting faced death calmly and courageously. One of the young people who succored the wounded in the quarter of the city where I was living at the time was called Anne. She was a very pretty girl of twenty-one, an excellent student and an accomplished dancer and athlete as well. She was, moreover, engaged to a man she deeply loved. Despite her parents' reminders of all the joy and happiness that life promised her she risked death daily during the air raids. She was well aware of the danger. Nor was there any question in her case of heroism or temerity. She simply did what she took to be her duty. The ironic outcome of this story is that the servant woman was killed in a cellar where she had been hiding while Anne survived the war safe and sound. This story obviously proves nothing, unless it might be that panic fear is far from being a certain indication of the instinct for preservation.

It is only apparently paradoxical that those in love with life are less afraid of death than those who live superficially. On a deeper psychological view, this is perfectly normal. As we shall show in Chapter IV, those whose lives have no meaning cannot give meaning to their death. They quite naturally fear an absurd death. But they are just as afraid of life and the risks it necessarily contains. Such men, when they find themselves in difficult circumstances, wish they had never been born. I have seen them condemn their parents for bringing them into the world and blaspheme God for creating a world of injustice and discord. But the authentically alive can readily see that death is not the end but the fulfillment of life. Since generosity was the very stuff of their lives why should they not consent generously to their deaths? This attitude is not inspired by fatalism or mysticism or even necessarily by hope for an afterlife. As an eminent theologian remarked to me one day, the fear of death is by no means the prerogative of unbelievers. There are believers who are terrified of death and unbelievers who ignore it—and of course the opposite is just as often the case. It is an error to think that faith delivers us from the fear of death or that the latter is the origin of religious faith. It is rather love of life that delivers us from the fear of death, and this love is found in believers and unbelievers alike.

We are obviously speaking here of an authentic love of life. Despite appearances, those who live selfishly cannot really love life. The thought that one day they will no longer be able to enjoy the pleasures which they think justify life gives rise to anguish. They are even more afraid of old age. They generally think of death as a relapse into nothingness. In such a state they will not be capable of enjoyment, but by the same token the desire to enjoy will no longer be present. They count on pleasure to distract them from an inevitable but hopefully distant fate. They consider old age so frightful because it leaves desire intact but takes away the means to satisfy it. A few years ago I knew such an old roué. He spent most of his life frequenting the haunts of pleasure. When old age had rendered him incapable of his accustomed enjoyments, he wept with rage and late in the evening would stand forlornly outside the illuminated façades of nightclubs and pleasure houses. He practiced an exhibitionism before schoolgirls that was more ridiculous and pitiful than dangerous to the virtue of the young students. This degenerate had an overwhelming fear of death whereas logically he should have greeted it as a release from his unhappiness. But this kind of person, far from loving life, is always a victim of neurotic conflicts. He is anxiety-ridden and just as afraid of life as he is of death. The frenetic pursuit of pleasure is an effort, often unconscious, to escape the anguish that tortures him.

It should be pointed out that we have been speaking only of extreme cases. For the ordinary man, the thought of death inspires a fear concomitant with his sensitivity and imaginative capacity. It is remarkable that many who are afraid of death as they imagine it accept it calmly in actuality. Those who have been involved in possibly fatal accidents say they experienced no fear while the danger lasted. Only afterwards, when they realize the danger they passed through, do they become frightened. This is because their imagination lets them see what might have happened had they not been so lucky. After such experiences, some men count on accidental death to spare them the terrors of death. But as soon as they entertain this possibility imaginatively they are afraid to take an airplane trip or even travel by automobile.

[3] THE DEATH OF OTHERS

Man is not only afraid of his own death. The death of others, particularly those we love or depend on materially or morally, can be just as agonizing. Some men, when they are young and healthy, give no thought to their own death, as though they didn't believe in it, and consequently they have no fear of it. But they worry about the death of their parents, children or other close ones.

Susan, thirty-eight years old, is married to a man her own age and has three children. She lives in perpetual fear of her husband's death. If he is a few minutes late coming home from work, she imagines he has had an accident and becomes terribly upset. When he does come home, instead of rejoicing that he is unharmed, she reproaches him for the fear he has caused her. When he is not feeling well she diagnoses (with the help of a medical dictionary) symptoms of leukemia and other fatal diseases. The thought of her husband's death even haunts her dreams. She sees herself in mourning, attending his funeral, accepting the condolences of her friends and relatives. When she suddenly wakes up it is some time before she can calm down and convince herself that her husband is well. Although a well educated woman, she is constantly consulting fortune-tellers and astrologists about her husband's longevity.

It would be wrong to conclude that Susan's fear is inspired by exceptional love for her husband. It is clear from her dreams and spontaneous reflections that she thinks of herself almost exclusively. "What would I do without him?" "How would I raise the children?" "I would be so alone, so alone." Occasionally, especially in her dreams, she quite clearly desires her husband's death, if for no other reason than that it would enable her to cut a fine figure in mourning. Sometimes, almost unconsciously, she poses before a mirror with a black shawl and observes that the role suits her perfectly; then she is overcome with remorse for having permitted herself such thoughts.

Pierre, a bachelor of forty-five, lives with his mother. He is an only son; his father died when he was an adolescent, and he has since been coddled by a too-possessive mother. Since he came of age she has constantly urged him to marry, but as soon as he shows interest in a woman his mother rejects her. Pierre is not fooled by this but he always gives in. He tells himself that since his mother has done so much for him he has no right to leave her alone. He could bring his wife to live with her but he knows that this would create an impossible situation. In recent years he has been increasingly bothered by the thought of his mother's death, although she is in good health. Each time she goes out he imagines countless dangers besetting her. If he notices that she is a little tired, he becomes unreasonably concerned. His mother, for

her part, profits by her son's fears to make him more dependent on her. She refuses to let him go out with friends and
insists that he be with her whenever he is not working. Pierre
sincerely believes that this fear of his mother's death is motivated by his love for her as well as by the fact that, since he
has always lived with her, his life would be meaningless if
he had to live alone. He knows, of course, that his mother
will die in the near future; he knows, too, that the older he
gets the more dependent he becomes upon her. But this does
not mitigate his present fears. He consulted a psychotherapist,
who quickly saw that Pierre realized, even though he didn't
admit it, that his insipid life was due to his mother's possessive love. Thus, unconsciously, he was really afraid that his
mother wouldn't die soon enough for him to get married and
lead a normal life. But, again unconsciously, he feels guilty
for desiring his mother's death. His obsessive fear of her death
and his solicitous concern for her welfare are explained by his
desire to rid himself of this guilt.

These examples do not point to any systematic conclusions.
Not all who fear the death of their loved ones are egocentrics
like Susan; nor does their fear always conceal a repressed
desire for the death of the person in question, as in Pierre's
case. Fear of someone's death cannot be attributed to such
equivocal and neurotic motives unless that fear is obviously
excessive and without objective foundation. Even then, we
should beware of generalizing and study each case in particular. Nothing is more dangerous and scientifically unorthodox
than drawing general theories from the observations made by
depth psychologists.

Fear of the death of others can be perfectly normal. A
mother who is excessively apprehensive about a sick child
certainly does not desire, monstrous exceptions apart, the

death of her child, either consciously or unconsciously. It would be equally absurd to accuse her of egoism. To be sure, she realizes how unhappy she would be if the child died. But she does everything she can to save the child, not to spare herself unhappiness but because she loves it and it is in the nature of love to desire the welfare of the one we love. And life, despite the difficulties and risks inherent in it, is spontaneously considered by each of us as one of the greatest, if not the greatest, values, the precondition for all others.

When an airplane crash has been reported, it is normal to be uneasy if a member of the family has to fly shortly afterwards. Otherwise would be to totally lack imagination. It little matters that "statistically" the odds are against two successive accidents. In short, whenever the danger of death of a loved one is real, or at least probable, fear is a very natural human reaction. Lack of it would not be a sign of superior emotional control or courage but a sign of indifference and insensitivity, or, at worst, a sign of a pathological absence of imagination. It is also normal for such fear to be greater in times of war or natural catastrophes.

The following case throws light on another psychological phenomenon. A woman whose husband had been conscripted for military service greatly feared that he would die. "Since I am a believer," she said, "I know he would go directly to heaven and be much happier there than on earth. But since I am afraid, isn't that proof that my love is not disinterested enough, that I am thinking more of my unhappiness without him than of his happiness in heaven?" We shouldn't be too concerned about the "absolute purity" of our motives. Such scruples may be evidence of a demanding faith, but they are much more likely to indicate a psychological aberrance. Love for another which included no love of self would not be human; in fact, it is psychologically impossible. When

Christ promulgated the commandment of fraternal love he did not say we must love others by renouncing love of self. He said: "Love others *as* you love yourselves." I have had ample opportunity in my professional career to observe that those who are incapable of loving others, who are at odds with their environments, were the very ones who did not sufficiently love themselves. Those who show hostility toward others are generally unconsciously determined to destroy themselves. Only after they are reconciled with themselves will they be able to love others.

Normal people rarely experience fear at the thought of their parents' death, still less of their grandparents' death. They take care of them when they are sick and are saddened by their suffering. But, whether they admit it or not, they feel that it is in the order of things for old people to die before the young. When a parent dies in old age we often feel a sorrow not unlike that experienced when someone dear to us goes on a long voyage. Only a neurotic would pretend to be inconsolable in such a circumstance.

But the case is quite different when death threatens someone our own age or, worse still, younger than we are. An old friend who had suffered much when his mother and later his wife died, told me one day as his son was fighting for his life on a hospital bed, "The fear of the death of one's own son, even if one is not particularly close to him, is unspeakably more painful than the fear of even the most passionately loved wife's death." This is partially explained by the instinctive desire all men have to survive in their children; in addition, we find the death of young people scandalous, a violation of the natural order. Only the non-accidental deaths of old people seem to be in perfect conformity with the natural order and do not provoke reactions of fear and anguish in normal people.

As we have said, when we fear that someone may die it is most often because we love that person and desire the supreme natural good which is life for him. But we sometimes experience an agonizing fear of another's death for less altruistic motives—because, for example, we see in his death a harbinger or a reminder of our own death. I am thinking here of a man I once knew who was a great lover of life's pleasures. Although he was already advanced in years, he told me he never thought about his death and for that reason never had any fear of it. But when three of his friends died in rapid succession, he changed his attitude. Afterwards, whenever he learned that someone his age or younger was sick, he would be afraid that that person might die, even if he had not known him particularly well. He began to read the obituary notices in the newspapers before anything else. His friends were surprised that he had suddenly developed such an interest in others and such a fear of death. In fact, all he was afraid of was his own death, but he refused to admit this. Despite himself, he often felt his pulse. He asked his doctor friends to control his blood pressure. He would often opine that he could well have cancer and was greatly displeased if he was not contradicted. One day his family discovered that he was secretely consuming a great variety of rare drugs. Still he refused to admit that he was afraid of his own death and continued in his life of pleasure-seeking.

[4]   THE FEAR OF COLLECTIVE DEATH

This form of fear is characterized by dread of one's own death together with those of others. Until recently, this kind of fear was in most cases geographically limited. War, even when gas or intensified bombing was used, never threatened more than a city or at most a region. People of Normandy, whose cities and provinces were destroyed in 1944, have told me that the fear they experienced then was much greater than the fear one knows when confronted with an individual danger. They thought a general cataclysm had befallen them, that no one had any chance of escaping. But at the same time they hoped that Auvergne and Savoie, where they had sent their children, would be spared. Those who are suddenly awakened by an earthquake fear for themselves and others but they do not think that the whole world is threatened. In fact they can legitimately hope that if they succeed in getting away from the threatened area quickly enough they will be safe.

For some time now, scientists have noted a progressive cooling of the earth and they predict that one day life here will no longer be possible. Since this will take place in the distant future, it is not felt as an immediate threat. Even a sidereal collision, which astronomists believe is inevitable and which will certainly pulverize our planet, does not cause us real fear. Such phenomena are beyond the imagination of the ordinary man.

Certain religious sects periodically announce the end of the world by direct divine intervention. The first great religious expectation of the end of the world, in which all of Christendom seems to have believed, took place just before the year 1000. But there is no evidence that this expectation generated universal terror. Of course, preachers profited by the circumstances to incite repentance and a change of life and stressed the more terrifying aspects of the last judgment. But joyful hope in the immediate return of the Savior seems to have been the dominant attitude. An extraordinary number of beautiful churches and cathedrals were built, for Christians wanted the world to be worthy to receive the Master. But Christ's return and the consequent end of the world did not take place in 1000. Since then, every dramatic age has had its prophets and "illuminati" who have predicted the precise date of the world's end, usually with Biblical evidence to support their claims. And there have always been those who believed the prophecies. In modern times the Adventists and other Pentecostal sects specialize in the discernment of signs and prophecies of the apocalyptic end of the world. They have already set several dates in the twentieth century. Each time, the credulous are seized with fear and give away their worldly goods in the hope that they will be numbered among the elect while all others go to eternal punishment. It is remarkable that despite so many disillusionments each prophet of doom continues to find followers. It may be concluded from this that mankind's expectation of a collective death has its roots in the collective unconscious. This seems to correspond to one of the archetypes of Jungian psychology. This is not unique to Christianity; it is the spiritual patrimony of other civilizations as well.

"Civilizations now know that they are mortal," wrote Paul Valéry. But since the Fifties, the fear of collective death has taken on an entirely now form which is no longer related to the expectation of a last judgment, the possible collision of the stars or the future cooling of the earth. Since the beginning of the insane race for nuclear superiority, the fate of mankind is in the hands of men themselves. What took place on a relatively modest scale in 1945 at Hiroshima and Nagasaki furnishes us with a very concrete image of how the destruction of the earth and its inhabitants could come about. The bombs stockpiled by the Americans and Russians could end life on our planet in a few hours. Nor is the production of nuclear energy for industrial and peaceful uses entirely without danger. Like Prometheus, men today have succeeded in unleashing forces they cannot totally master.

Thus the fear of collective death is far more justified than ever before. Some optimists trust in the wisdom of heads of state, hoping that the famous "balance of terror" will prevent not only a final cataclysm but also the "classic" type of war. But the pessimists have a point when they say that an accident, an error in calculation or a Nero-type madness in one of those who control the button could unleash a universal holocaust. The hot line linking Moscow and the White House is a feeble guarantee, especially in view of the fact that a monopoly on nuclear arms will not long remain in the hands of the two great powers. And who can guarantee that men far less scrupulous than our present leaders, men like Hitler and Stalin, will not accede to power at some future date?

In most of the countries of Western Europe, men are rationally convinced of the great danger represented by nuclear weapons. But most of them don't seem to be especially disturbed. Perhaps they lack imagination. Yet, on the other hand, I have heard people in West Germany say, "Why should we work so hard to erect permanent buildings and save for the future when the chances for a future are so slim?" Some of my patients have refused to marry or have children since, they argue, it is clear that their offspring would suffer the horrors of a thermonuclear war. This is a modern version of the fear that neurotics of all times have experienced when confronted with the risks and responsibilities of life. Still, it seems that more normal people today are affected by this fear of collective death, at least unconsciously. This is at least a partial explanation of the disarray of our times, which is expressed in gratuitous crime, vandalism, eroticism and the accelerated pace of life. Even modern music and dances seem to express the despair of a humanity that no longer believes in its own future. Unlike the Adventists and other prophets who expect the end of the world through divine intervention, most men today are not inclined to await, in prayer and penance, the nuclear destruction of life. They are not about to change their hearts but rather are intent upon enjoying whatever passing pleasure life affords them. They hope, more or less consciously, to repress their fear in distractions.

It is psychologically significant that the fear of death by thermonuclear war or accident is greatest in those countries that for the moment have a quasi-monopoly on this frightful weapon. Our knowledge of Russia is admittedly indirect. But from what we are able to garner, it appears that the Soviet leaders are bad psychologists because they fail to realize that the immediate effect of their boasting is necessarily to increase fear.

In the United States the fear of collective death is often overtly neurotic in character. This explains much of the recent absurd behavior of this fundamentally democratic and pacific nation. The witch hunts of the McCarthy period, the propaganda for a preventive nuclear war against Russia and, more recently, against China, and the millions of dollars spent to assure hypothetical protection against an atomic attack are so many expressions of the fear affecting a whole people. Bomb shelters, for example, are constructed at great expense although it is obvious that they would be useless in case of war. Incidents of criminality, eroticism, abuse of alcohol and drugs seem more rampant in the United States than elsewhere. Today the stronger and richer a nation is, the greater is its insecurity.

[5]   NEUROTIC FEAR

Several of the "cases" we have analyzed above are clearly neurotic in character. Neurosis is an important element of

the kind of fear, often having little or no objective motivation, which many people experience when they reflect on the
death of others. It remains to clarify further the role of neurosis in certain especially negative forms of the fear of death.

Neurotic fear characteristically is either without objective
motivation or highly disproportionate to it. The victims themselves frequently admit that they don't know what they are
afraid of or, especially, why they are afraid. Often their fear
develops into real anguish, preventing them from living, acting and even sleeping in peace. It is frequently complicated
by somatic difficulties, such as a slow pulse (sometimes to the
point where the heart seems to have stopped beating), suffo-
cation, asthmatic attacks, etc.

Renée, a woman of thirty-five, never dreams of anything
but railroad or automobile accidents. When she has to travel
she surrounds herself with multiple precautions which she
knows full well would not protect her in case of an accident.
She does not consider herself superstitious yet confesses that
she would die of fear if she had to travel in an automobile
without a St. Christopher medal. She decided not to marry
because the continual thought of her future death would make
such a commitment ridiculous. When she did marry, as a result of parental pressure, she categorically refused to have
children. Why give life when we know perfectly well that
death triumphs in the end? Only intermittently does she forget her fear of death to enjoy life a little, but she is soon
overcome with remorse. Early in her marriage she unex-
pectedly experienced a very pleasurable orgasm. She interpreted this loss of consciousness as a foretaste of death and
since that time has stubbornly refused to take pleasure in
sexual relations. A believing Catholic, she feels that monastic
life (the essence of which is for her less the praise and service

of God than asceticism and penance, i.e., death to the world)
is the only life to have any meaning. But, as is typical of
neurotics who are confronted with their stated ideals and convictions, she has never seriously thought of entering religious
life, on the pretext that she is unworthy.

George, a thirty-year-old teacher, was overcome with an
agonizing fear of death while attending his grandfather's funeral. Suddenly he saw himself in a coffin surrounded by mourning relatives. Until then, he had been periodically stricken with
anxiety—"without any motive," as he said, which is to say,
without conscious motivation—and in addition had had great
difficulties in adjusting to his profession and to social life in
general. But he had never been afraid of death. In fact, he
had never consciously thought about it. Now he thinks of
nothing else. In his dreams death appears to him in the imagery of the medieval cathedrals—terrifying, mocking and
threatening. He wakes up in the middle of the night scream-
ing. He often awakens his wife to listen to his heart and assure
him that it is still beating. George has had several fainting
spells, but medical specialists have been unable to detect the
slightest physical problem. He can offer no explanation for
his fear, although he admits that he is not too enamored of life,
that he has never been very happy and that, even before his
grandfather's death, he often wished he were dead. On two
occasions he has attempted suicide. This kind of paradoxical
behavior is quite common among neurotics. They precipitate
themselves toward that which they fear. After each fainting
spell and each attempted suicide George was terrified imagin-
ing what his fate might have been if he had really died. In
vain did his family, unbelievers like himself, try to assure him
that there is nothing after death. If he really died everything
would be over; he would return to nothingness, pure and sim-

ple. But this nothingness was precisely what he was afraid of. He thought of it as a hole, a terrible abyss. He said, in self-mockery, that he could not believe in God or heaven but did believe in hell. One day, when his anguish was more unbearable than usual, he decided to visit a priest secretly. He went to confession and communion. For some days he was at peace; then his anguish returned. His doctor, after trying various drugs to no avail, advised psychotherapy. It became clear that his agonizing fear of death was the crystallization of a nervous state originating in his frustrated and loveless childhood.

From a psychological point of view, the neurotic fear of death is never an isolated fact; nor can it be isolated. It is a manifestation of the neurotic personally as a whole. Neither the consolations of religion nor the power of argument can prevail against it. The whole person must be treated, frequently for a long period of time. Often enough, the real problem is not the fear of death at all, but some unconscious psychological conflict going back to the patient's childhood or adolescence. Once the psychic energies that have been inhibited by neurosis are liberated, the fear of death vanishes as though by magic.

[6] THE FEAR OF HELL

It was long believed that punishment was a particularly efficacious means of education. If a child misbehaved, its mother or nurse threatened to "tell everything to father." The boogy man, Santa Claus and a host of other mythological figures were called upon to make children toe the line. Religion itself was thought to contribute to the education of children and the maintenance of the social order because its teachings contained terrible threats of punishment for the "wicked." I have heard altogether reasonable men say, "If the Bible didn't teach the existence of Hell, we would have to invent it to preserve social order and peace." We have only to look at the paintings and sculptures of our cathedrals to realize the primordial role threats of hellfire played in the education of our ancestors.

Nor is it necessary to go back to the Middle Ages. In the very recent past, Lenten preachers and parochial missionaries hoped to convert the lukewarm and sinful with detailed descriptions of the torments of Hell. Fire, cauldrons of boiling oil, and Satan and his demon helpers were taken as fundamental religious truths. Most ministers of religion today follow the general direction of modern pedagogy and no longer believe in the moral efficacy of fear. Thus they no longer preach on Hell. Yet the concept continues to haunt many imaginations. Certain Protestant sects such as the Adventists and Jehovah's Witnesses still hold the fear of Hell to be the best means of converting sinners. The same is true of certain segments of Catholicism. I once heard a preacher in a respected retreat house claim that he knew that all the "wicked" (among them those who did not share his conservative political ideas) would be victims of eternal hellfire. On another occasion I actually saw the presumably enlightened author of one of these spiritual exercises enter into a sort of ecstasy and, with hands raised to heaven, shout, "I see him. . . . I see him. . . . How horrible. . . . He is burning in Hell. . . . The devil sneers and attacks. . . ." I later learned that the subject of this horrifying vision was a recently deceased archbishop of Paris who was guilty, in the eyes of the integralists, of favoring social reform in Leon Blum's government in 1936. It is astonishing that illuminism of this sort is still effective in a skeptical age. I know any number of educated men whose lives have been changed by meditation on the horrors of Hell. But in other cases serious neurotic anxieties result.

Sects of illuminati (as well as certain backward regions where religious life is always dominated by Jansenist theology) apart, the fear of Hell still plays a fairly important role in the psychic lives of well educated men and women who live in dechristianized areas. This is particularly true of neurotics, whether believers or not.

Maurice is a militant atheist and bitterly anticlerical. Suffering from anxiety and other psychic troubles, he underwent psychotherapy. He was haunted by the fear of death and troubled by "ridiculous" nightmares dominated by the imagery of Hell. The humor of the situation struck him: "If I don't believe in God would I be stupid enough to believe old wives tales about Satan and Hell?" Yet he does believe and is terribly afraid. Consciously he is an atheist, but ancient archetypes are at work in his unconscious. In Maurice's case, his fear of Hell ceased only when he adopted a positive religion of love.

We should resist the temptation to draw an apologetic argument from this particular case. Other neurotics get rid of their fear of Hell and still remain atheists, and religious neurotics often lose their faith in God along with their fear of Hell. Belief, like unbelief, can be neurotic in origin and disappear after the neurosis has been cured. Again, both can be expressions of a healthy psyche and remain intact when neurotic fears have been liquidated.

As a rule, well educated and dedicated Christians are least afraid of Hell. They do not take all the pious(?) imagery about Hell literally. If out of fidelity to the traditional teachings of their Church they do not explicitly deny the reality of Hell, they at least entertain a purified, highly spiritual idea of it. But it is significant that even these Christians are plagued by thoughts of Hell when the moment of death approaches. They understand Hell as the frightening possibility of being separated from God, in whom they believe, and this perspective is as fearsome to them as the cruder conceptions of Hell are to others.

[7] SOME CAUSES OF THE FEAR OF DEATH

A neurotic fear of death is most often the expression of a general anxiety whose real causes are unconscious and originate with the traumas of adolescence, childhood or birth. Such fear is no more justified than claustrophobia or agoraphobia. But as we have often noted in this chapter, not all who are tortured by the fear of their own death or those of others are neurotics, unless we consider the whole human race neurotic.

This universal fear seems to me to furnish a supplementary argument against those who affirm with Freud the existence of a death instinct, an argument that should carry some weight at least with biologists and psychologists. Normally an instinct tends toward the realization of its end, unless it is inhibited by repressions or other barriers that are difficult to surmount. But there is no reason to assume that all who fear death have repressed their death instinct, which Freud considered in his last years the most fundamental instinct of all. If men are so afraid of death it would seem to be because life rather than death is most important to them. Thus it may be unequivocally affirmed that the principal cause of the fear of death is the life instinct, while death is the enemy of this authentically fundamental instinct.

In this sense the fear of death is perfectly natural. It is unnatural when it becomes an obstacle to life instead of serving and protecting it. This is obviously the case with neurotic fear and several other kinds of fear of death we have analyzed. The principal cause of this seems to be the excessive individualism of modern man, at least in the civilized countries of the West. This is not true, as we have pointed out, of more primitive peoples whose individual consciousness is less pronounced. Even in the old civilizations of the East, relatively little importance is given to individual destiny. This undoubtedly explains why the Chinese, Vietnamese and Japanese (the most Westernized of Asiatic peoples) do not hesitate to die *en masse* when their leaders so order. In the prosperous countries of the West we live more exclusively for ourselves and our sense of self-identity is more developed. Community bonds are becoming less and less binding. Frenchmen, for example, found it normal to risk their lives for their country in 1914. But that was not true during World War II. Only the Resistance succeeded, for a brief period, in inspiring a collective consciousness. The Germans, on the other hand, were far less individualistic than the French but, from what I have been able to observe in postwar Germany, recent prosperity has accelerated the process of individualization. Today, I have the impression that Germans would be no more disposed to sacrifice their individual lives for a collective cause than the French. Emmanuel Mounier wisely pointed out that "all pacifism based on the fear of death is a ferment of decomposition that usurps an unmerited prestige."

Nowhere does the fear of death seem to be as universal and pronounced as in the United States. The funeral rituals practiced there are particularly revealing. The famous novelist Evelyn Waugh cruelly but accurately satirized these practices in his novel, *The Loved One*. Cadavers are embalmed, painted and made the objects of ridiculous pomp that has nothing in common with the honor Christianity traditionally accorded the mortal remains of a soul that was considered immortal. Here it is solely a question of the deep fear death inspires in a people who are too endowed with the goods and comforts of this world. The death of others reminds us of our own death. And it is to exorcise this fear that corpses are made up to give the illusion of being alive.

Another cause of abnormal fear of death is the increasing materialism of Western civilization. I am not thinking here of the victories of dialectical materialism. Western man's psychic balance has been much more disturbed by that pragmatic materialism which is in reality endorsed by great numbers of men who intellectually profess the most elevated spiritual ideas. Given the fact that hedonism has become the supreme existential goal of life for so many, why shouldn't the prospect of having to renounce such enjoyment be considered frightening? But the widespread feeling of insecurity in the West, despite all our laws for social protection, constantly reminds us how precarious the hedonistic way of life is. In this psychological context, it is surprising that the fear of death and the neurotic anxiety caused by such fear are not more widespread. This tends to confirm the fact that, in the depths of his being, Western man is less civilized than appearances would indicate.

[8]   OVERCOMING THE FEAR OF DEATH

No man can live in a constant state of great fear. If we continually feared death our lives would soon become intolerable. We would no longer have either the strength or the desire to do anything, and anxiety would very likely drive us to insanity. Fortunately, the fear of death is not continuous; even neurotics enjoy more or less prolonged respites from it. The struggle against the fear of death is therefore in keeping with the inherent logic of life, although admittedly this struggle is more difficult than ever today. The more men become masters of the world of nature, the less they feel masters of themselves.

Man has always made an effort to conquer his fear of death. The West has long believed in the omnipotence of intelligence, and consequently almost all of the philosophers and moralists have sought remedy in rational argument. The ancient materialism of Epicurus and Lucretius, among others, was directly inspired by the desire to conquer the fear of death. They reasoned that if there were no god there could be no immortality either. Therefore, why should death be feared? Death will reduce man to the nothingness he was born of; it will necessarily put an end to suffering and evil as well as pleasure. Men would not fear death if they did not believe in Hell and vindictive gods. Despite its ingenuity, the materialistic argument does not seem to have obtained the expected results. Even today, as we have seen, materialists are no more exempt from the fear of death than those who believe in God's judgment.

The Stoics held that the fear of death was caused by man's emotions. Stoic philosophy was interested only in the soul; the body and other natural phenomena concerned it only insofar as they influenced the soul. Now, death is a natural event that is as inevitable as the fall of the rain or the movement of the stars. Therefore it is by nature something indifferent and not worth worrying about. One should live in the present and not be preoccupied about the length of one's life. But in order to do this, the imagination, which is the source of all harmful emotions, must be rigorously curbed. Stoic wisdom therefore recommends *ataraxia,* an emotionless state of tranquillity.

Spinoza also saw in the imagination the principal cause of our fear of death. Non-being, which according to him is the very condition of death, only exists in the imagination. Only being has real existence. To prevent the imagination from creating fictitious objects we must learn how to use our reason well. Spinoza offers the following example of a "good argument" that demonstrates, he thought, the inanity of our fear of death: "Either I am and therefore my essence is divine (and thus cannot die) or I am not and nothingness is in no way positive."

Schopenhauer is one of those modern philosophers whose influence has long been great. He has left his mark on Nietzsche and the existentialists, among others. Today he is rarely read, but his influence persists nonetheless. To overcome the fear of death and learn the art of living, Schopenhauer studied Buddhism as well as he could, given the conditions in the West of his time. He discovered that the cause of the fear of death was the will to live, a will that was for this reason altogether evil and was, moreover, absolutely unjustifiable. "We are basically something that should not be; thus it is normal that we one day cease to exist," he wrote. Schopenhauer held that the only reality that should be preserved was the species itself. The individual is by nature a temporal and ephemeral phenomenon. The unhappiness of man, who alone among living creatures refuses to be merely a member of the species and for this reason is afraid of death, derives from his intelligence. In fact this ego whose destruction by death we so much fear is nonexistent; it is a mere illusion and the idea of death is the rotten fruit of that illusion. We should bend every effort to identifying as completely as possible with our species. To the extent that we succeed we will overcome our fear of death, since the species cannot perish. If Schopenhauer were alive today he would very likely be afraid of death since the extinction of the human species, and all living species, has now entered the realm of possibility as a result of thermonuclear energy.

Idealism, the other great strand of modern philosophical thought, not only contests the reality of the individual but moreover asserts that the whole sensory world is an illusion. The only true reality is spirit, which cannot truthfully be represented as a thing. The laws governing the empirical universe are the work of the imagination and do not apply to the spirit. Thus we erroneously think of birth and death as though they were in some way expressions of being. In fact, they merely represent our way of thinking. According to Idealism, therefore, the only effective weapon against fear of death is to live in the spirit and have as little to do with the empirical world as possible. "When there is no time there can be no end of time," wrote Kant. That great master of modern Idealism taught that space and time were nothing more than *a priori* categories of the mind.

Existentialism also confronts the eternal problem of man's attitude toward death. Sartre and other existential atheists follow their German master, Martin Heidegger, on this question. Man is and must think of himself as a "being-toward-death." It is a basic mistake to think that he is made for life and that death is consequently scandalous. Self-consciousness cannot be separated from consciousness of one's death. Similarly, our awareness of others necessarily implies an awareness of their death. Life can only be considered normal by those who have neither self-consciousness nor consciousness of others. Since Heidegger insists upon the factitiousness of existence in much the same way as did the Stoics and Schopenhauer, we might expect him to deliver men from their fear of death. But he does not. He contends that an awareness of one's death and the resultant anxiety are equally natural to man. We can no more escape the anxiety of death than we can escape the human condition. Courage and lucidity, two "virtues" much appreciated by the Existentialists, consist in confronting this anxiety unflinchingly, because there is no honest way of avoiding it. Since Sartre and Heidegger consider death the most personal of man's possibilities, the authenticity of existence they wish to achieve necessarily implies lucid and courageous acceptance of death and the fear of death. Our unshakable certainty of death reveals the fragility, radical contingency and absurdity of existence. Sartre has one of his characters say: "Life is a story told by an idiot and it is precisely because death is inevitable and anxiety insurmountable that life is idiotic." No lie is admissible; the human condition is tragic. The essence of man, according to the existentialists, is his freedom. Confronted with death man has only two alternatives: either he can accept it and the anxiety that accompanies it, or he can try to distract himself. The acceptance of death implies that we constantly await it. The authentic man must live in constant anticipation of his death. All of our possibilities depend on death and by that token become impossibilities. Nowhere better than in his anxiety over death does man understand himself as nothingness. There is no deliverance from this situation; no one can help us; each of us is radically isolated in his own nothingness.

To my knowledge no Marxist thinker has seriously considered the problem of our fear of death. The problem orig-

inates with human subjectivity, and Marxists have always behaved as if all subjective problems were part of the deadly
heritage of capitalistic alienation which Communism is called
upon to transcend dialectically. Implicitly, Marxists very
nearly follow Schopenhauer's belief that individual existence
is of no importance. "Species" became the "collectivity" in
Marxist language. But there is some evidence that European
Marxists are becoming more individualistic. If that is the case,
they will not be able to avoid such "subjective" problems as
the fear of death much longer.

I do not propose to discuss the philosophical value of the
different schools of thought we have just reviewed. But I am
interested in their existential effectiveness. I have no doubt
that the various theories and maxims proposed were valuable
at least for their authors. But I have never known anyone
wrestling with the fear of death who found the slightest help
in Stoic *ataraxia,* or Schopenhauer's rejection of the will to
live, or the intellectual speculations of Spinoza and the Ide-
alists. I have known many who gave lip service to the courage
and lucidity recommended by the Existentialists, but unfortunately no one has ever succeeded in putting them into practice. In his books, Sartre himself admits to the overwhelming
anxiety he experiences when he reflects upon man's mortal
condition. It seems that his own philosophy cannot cure him
or help him confront the problem with courage and lucidity.
Because philosophical wisdom has failed here, most modern
men have recourse to two "techniques" that enable them to
live with their fear of death—escape and repression.

We have already mentioned the more-or-less magical rites
practiced in America and elsewhere that are intended to
conjure away the fear of death. We notice in countries with
a high standard of living that the abuse of alcohol and nar-

cotics and the frenetic pursuit of pleasure are so many efforts to dispel the fear of death. I have often interrogated *bon vivants* on the motives of their behavior. They frequently answer that they are looking for "oblivion," although they are generally not too specific about what they are trying to forget. Analysis showed that they were trying to forget their fear of death. But they realized that distractions provided a very superficial kind of forgetfulness. In order not to awaken the "forgotten" fear it is considered good taste never to mention death or the dead in social conversation. The subject is usually alluded to in such euphemistic expressions as, "He lived," "He went away," "He is no longer with us," "He passed on" and the like. Even military bulletins are inclined to speak of the "missing" rather than the dead.

Repression is, strictly speaking, caused by unconscious psychic mechanisms and is widespread in the Western world. We find evidence of it in people who say they never think of death or have no fear of it. I have often noticed that the more the fear of death is repressed the greater harm it does. The psychological process of repression never solves any problem. Like repressed instincts, repressed fears continue to act nonetheless, only now they are beyond the pale of rational control and, consequently, much more destructive.

In insisting on the ineffectiveness of repression and the harmfulness of efforts to forget the fear of death, I am not siding with preachers and editors of pious books who recommend that we think about death constantly and live as though we might die at any moment. If we constantly thought about death it would be impossible to live as we should. As we pointed out, it is impossible for most men (whether or not they are believers) to think about death and not fear it. And it is psychologically difficult, if not impossible, to do anything creative when we are in the grip of strong fear. While wholly realizing his mortality, the normal man only occasionally reflects upon death—when a member of his family dies or he witnesses an accident or reads about some catastrophe in the papers. I have received the confidences of many men who narrowly escaped political death. While awaiting execution, some of them lived in constant states of anxiety; some lost their reason; others bore the neurotic stigmata of their anxiety for years afterwards. Still others managed to live as though no danger existed. They read, wrote and learned foreign languages. Yet they were just as attached to life as those who were afraid. Indeed more so, for it is probable that it was precisely their intense desire to live that enabled them to overcome their natural fear of death. Their strong life instinct made a death they *knew* to be imminent seem *unbelievable*.

It is my conviction that an intense love of life is the best and perhaps the only effective antidote against the fear of death. There is no need to repress fear or forget that we are mortal. But we can realize that we might die at any moment and yet live as though we were never going to die. I know many men, both men of action and intellectuals, who have honestly succeeded in living this apparent contradiction. They succeed because they do not repress their life instincts. Some masterpieces of art and literature, it is true, have been inspired by the fear of death. But more often, men who knew they were mortal but did not existentially fear death have been the artisans of human progress. Sublimation of our fear of death is the only real solution to the problem.

Contrary to what one might think, it is not only young men, with their futures before them, who successfully sublimate their fears of death. Old people succeed equally well. One of my dear friends, Mark, is approaching eighty and has begun undertakings that would normally take years to realize. Not that he resembles the greedy man in the evangelical parable who built granaries and amassed riches as though he were going to live forever—Mark is more like a builder of the earth. As a believing Christian he is prepared to meet his judge and redeemer. But his love of life is strong enough to enable him to sublimate the fear of death which he, like all men, experiences.

We shall have more to say on this existentially important problem in the chapter entitled "The Meaning of Death."

III

Suicide and Voluntary Death

*There is but one truly serious
philosophical problem, and that
is suicide.* —ALBERT CAMUS

C AMUS' words express the attitude of those who think
that life has no meaning, that death is the crowning point
of the absurdity of existence. Camus' position had already
been articulated by the great Romantic poet, Novalis: "The
philosophical act par excellence," he wrote, "is suicide. This
is the beginning of all philosophy." What Novalis, Camus
and other pessimistic philosophers want to explain is not suicide as such but the fact that most men do not commit suicide.
Because death is inevitable, human initiative is doomed to
failure. Suicide at least enables us to escape the absurd fatality of the human condition because then we choose the hour
and the means of our death. "What is called a reason for living is also an excellent reason for dying," Camus writes. This
means that no matter what man does, whether he lives or
dies, he can never avoid the absurdity of his destiny.

[I]   THE TEMPTATION OF SUICIDE

Suicide seems to occur with relative frequency at all levels of society, although it is more conspicuous among civilized peoples. It is judged differently in different ages and civilizations. The importance attached to the individual destiny of man is an important factor in these judgments. In decadent societies, where social bonds are weak, the individual generally considers himself the absolute master of his life and believes that he has the right to dispose of it as he sees fit. In such societies, suicides are more frequent and less scandalous. This was the case in the Roman Empire, for example, at least in the higher echelons of society. Such outstanding men as Seneca and Marcus Aurelius recommended suicide and followed their own advice. It was also the case during the epoch of triumphant individualism toward the end of the nineteenth century. On the other hand, suicide was considered a heinous crime and was rarely practiced during the Christian ages of the West. Then, life was thought to belong not to the individual but to God, who alone had the right to dispose of it—at least theoretically. It is interesting to note that Christian morality judged suicide far more severely than homicide and in fact still does. Many theologians have justified war, duelling, capital punishment and other forms of homicide but, to my knowledge, none has tried to justify suicide. This shows how far such writers as Novalis and Camus are from the Christian perspective.

In the great Oriental civilizations—Japan, China and India—the awareness of belonging to an ethnic collectivity predominates over self-awareness. This explains why suicide inspires no fear in these countries and is even held in high respect, especially when it is socially justified. But since I am writing as a psychologist, I shall limit my remarks to the world I know best, which is the West.

In attempting to understand the psychology of suicide, our inquiry and observations are necessarily restricted to those who have failed in the attempt. It is significant that they themselves are often quite unable to explain clearly the mental process which led them to take such a definitive step. When they tried to kill themselves they were not necessarily more depressed or despairing than usual. We might note too that they often make several attempts before they succeed. But I have met few who were happy to have escaped a premature death or showed gratitude toward those who saved them, often at the risk of their own lives. A young woman who tried to drown herself in the Seine was saved by a man who was brave enough to dive, fully clothed, into the wintry waters. But the woman he saved, far from thanking him and admiring his courage, treated him like an imbecile. When she learned that he had risked death to save her, she replied, "That will teach him to interfere with other peoples' business."

In addition to the testimony of those who have failed in their attempts to commit suicide, another source of information is the letters left by those who succeeded. However, their sincerity is not always beyond reproach. Many men attach great importance to the image others have of them. Even those who do not believe in an afterlife nonetheless think they will live on in some way such that the opinions of others will still matter to them. Thus they often embellish and "romanticize" their motives for suicide. Before Robert, age twenty-five, tried to kill himself with a revolver, he wrote letters to his parents, his fiancée and several friends in a very Camus-like style. He spoke of leaving an absurd life without regret, declared that a death freely chosen was a beautiful thing and exhorted others to follow his example. But soon after he had failed in his purpose, it was revealed that he had stolen money from his company and was unable to repay it. He attempted suicide to avoid prison and dishonor, but in the eyes of others he wanted his death to have "metaphysical" meaning. Others who attempt suicide are subjectively sincere but often fail to realize the unconscious motives underlying their conscious ones. With these reservations, it remains true that posthumous letters are of valuable help in exploring the psychology of those who give up life's battle.

It is difficult if not impossible to establish statistics in this matter. I am in no position to affirm that most men have at one time or another in their lives been tempted to commit suicide. But I do know in light of my experience that a very large number of those who have confided in me had been seriously tempted. I should point out, however, that these were, in almost all cases, well educated and rather complicated persons. It is therefore probable that simpler men who are closer to nature and whose life instincts are consequently less inhibited do not suffer this temptation. In the cases I have observed closely, however, the relative frequency of desire and attempts to take one's life do not permit us to draw the conclusion that a death instinct exists. Depth psychologists know that cultural factors generally play an inhibiting role with respect to the instincts. The sexual instinct, for example, is not nearly so "pure" in an intellectual as in a peasant. The instinct of self-preservation is likewise more easily inhibited in the former than the latter.

Here is how Paul Valéry analyzed his own attempt to commit suicide during a sojourn in London: "Was it the fog of the city, the mists of the Thames or boredom and disgust which, in the incontinence of the late hours, made me despairingly aware of the paltry character of the work I had undertaken to support myself in London. Everything seemed to be bereft of anything that could make life interesting, so that evening I resolved to do away with myself. . . . I had chosen hanging as the way I would die. . . . I had already entered the room where I intended taking my life and knotted the cord that I would soon put around my neck, when my eyes fell upon a yellow-covered, paperbound book which chance had placed on the floor beneath me. Why did I open the book? Why did I read it? In my vacant state, my gestures seemed to belong to a somnambulist, to someone else. . . . After I had read a few lines I was suddenly seized with a fit of laughter so hysterical, so loud—I can still hear it— that suddenly I felt liberated, delivered, disenchanted . . . that terrible laugh saved me." But for that mad laugh, France would have been deprived of one of her greatest poets.

[2]   COWARDLY SUICIDE

Newspapers frequently report the suicides of elderly persons, generally caused by extreme material misery, often combined with an equally extreme moral misery in the form of feelings of loneliness, abandonment and uselessness. Consider the old couple whose lives had been centered on their only son. When he left home and eventually stopped writing they lost all interest in life. They had no religious faith, no friends. Because they feared to hurt one another, they dared not talk about their unique common preoccupation, their son. Thus they lived in almost complete silence. Furthermore, they were not well off materially. One evening, one of them turned on the gas, without any apparent protest on the part of the other. The next morning the odor of gas attracted a neighbor's attention. The old couple was found dead, dead because they had no reason to live.

Confronted with such dramas of misery and loneliness, we can scarcely be surprised. Nor can we speak of cowardice. We only feel pity. It is regrettable that parents should be so exclusively dependent on their children. But this is not unusual in the case of an only child. It is even more regrettable when the object of such love proves to be ungrateful, but again this is not unusual. The weight of such possessive love is difficult to bear. When great material misery is the cause of suicide, we have more reason to blame society rather than the victims. In any case, it is psychologically understandable that the life instinct should weaken and even fail altogether in those who have lost their strength and reason for living.

On the other hand, there are many cases where suicide is motivated by cowardice, by a lack of courage to assume the normal responsibilities of life. I must warn the reader not to read any moral accusation into this objective observation. What is objectively cowardly may be subjectively motivated by factors that in no way involve the moral responsibility of the individual. The psychologist never has the right to rely on superficial evidence. In noting that so-and-so acts like a coward when confronted with the demands of life, he must ask himself: why is he cowardly? One is never cowardly or courageous from birth. And rarely do we become so solely because of our own fault or merit. The case we shall now analyze reveals a person who lacked courage in difficult life circumstances and fled his responsibilities. But he had been over-protected as an only son and, consequently, his cowardice was not entirely his own fault. His sense of self was not adequately structured and he exaggerated the importance of the image others had of him. He was the way he was because circumstances independent of his will had prevented him from acquiring a normal sense of self-confidence.

Francis, a fifty-year-old pharmacist, wanted to improve the rather mediocre material situation of his family. Following the advice of experts, he invested in real estate. He lacked experience in this kind of business and soon fell victim to the dishonesty of his associates. Not only did he not make a fortune, he lost nearly all of his savings. Heavily in debt, he was forced to sell his pharmacy. Still, his situation was not altogether hopeless. He soon found employment in a friend's business. Moreover, his wife and children accepted his failure with good grace, even though they had advised against his speculations. But Francis did not have the courage to accept his loss of prestige and begin again. He took a large dose of poison, which he had set aside before he sold his pharmacy, and died. This man loved his family and knew to what difficult circumstances his death would abandon them. But his cowardice and vanity were stronger than his love.

Charles, an engineer, was the father of a large family and a respected man in his community. He fell in love with his young secretary, the daughter of his best friend, and took her as his mistress. He bitterly reproached himself for having seduced her, deceived his wife and betrayed his friend. When he confided his embarrassing problem to me I had the clear impression that he was maliciously enjoying his guilty conscience. He boasted of loving two women at once and leading an apparently successful double life. He said most men he knew would be incapable of such a feat. But he was terribly upset when he learned that his young mistress had become pregnant. He was genuinely sorry for her, but it was rather his own dishonor that frightened him. It was impossible for the two to hide the event from their respective families. Charles did not feel courageous enough to face the complicated circumstances of his life. He felt that suicide was the only way out of his dilemma. He raced his powerful sports car into a huge rock, was thrown into a river, and drowned. Like Francis, Charles could not have been ignorant of the desperate situation he was leaving for both his family and his mistress. He was, moreover, an extremely vain man. In a letter he wrote just before he died, Charles called attention to the similarity between his despair and that of Scobie, the celebrated hero of Graham Greene's novel, *The Heart of the Matter*.

Having written several bad checks and been a party to various swindles, Philip was disowned by his parents. He had no money with which to pursue his studies and no professional competence. For a time, he earned a meager living by stealing. He tried to ingratiate himself with criminals but found that he had no stomach for their way of life. His future looked so bleak that he decided on suicide. One night he cut his wrists with a razor blade. He was discovered, near death, on a park bench. He recovered, but things continued to go badly, and for a period of some months he had thoughts of hanging, drowning and various other means of killing himself. But in the end his will to live, however weakened, triumphed. He overcame his feelings of shame and pride and went to see the chaplain of a student group he had once belonged to. The chaplain helped him find employment and living quarters. Today, fifteen years after this difficult time in his life, Philip is a successful and happy man. He is thankful that he did not have the courage to commit suicide and readily agrees that no situation is desperate enough to justify it.

As Philip's case indicates, although some have recourse to suicide because they cannot face the demands and responsibilities of life, others resist the temptation to commit suicide because they are afraid of death. The material and moral conditions of their lives may seem hopeless, and they may feel that life is an intolerable burden, but the fear of death frightens them even more. We may suppose that even in instances of this kind the life instinct is active. It is, of course, regrettable for a man to continue to live only because he lacks the courage to commit suicide. But all things considered, this kind of cowardice is more natural than the other.

[3] NEUROTIC SUICIDE

It is not easy to give a perfectly satisfactory definition of the "normal man." The difference between the normal and the neurotic is more a question of degree than of essence. But we may generally define the "normal" as those who live in approximate harmony with their basic instincts. Not that the normal man follows all of his instincts blindly. For a long time, moralists protested the absolute instinctual freedom recommended by psychoanalysts—particularly with regard to the sexual instinct, which Freud and his school were believed to insist upon. That Freud, in his passionate struggle against taboos and the repression of the libido, often spoke in an equivocal manner and thus exposed himself to this kind of objection is undeniable. It is even more undeniable that the popularizers of Freudian theories drew extreme conclusions from the hypotheses that Freud himself had only tentatively elaborated. By establishing a thesis on the basis of an unverified hypothesis, they recommended, in effect, that their patients live according to their instincts and condemned all restraint and control of them as forms of repression.

We do not share this conception of instinctual freedom. Man cannot achieve human normality by acting like an animal. The instincts, of course, should not be repressed, as this will almost inevitably cause serious neurotic conflicts. On the other hand, the instincts should not be the sole standards of our life. In evolving to the human sphere, what Teilhard de Chardin calls the noosphere, man did not cease to remain an integral part of the biosphere. Nonetheless, what is vital in him must in some sense be *spiritualized*. In animals, instinct is at the service of the species as much as the individual, an individual that is still embryonic. Only in man can we legitimately speak of individuality, so much so that at some periods of his development he seems to have forgotten that he belongs to the human race. If man let himself be guided solely by his instincts, he would risk doing serious harm to the species of which he is a part. This is because his instincts serve primarily the individual. It follows that even man's most basic instincts must in certain circumstances give way to demands other than the good of the individual, toward which they naturally tend. Life is the most precious of individual goods, and yet there are circumstances in which man must sacrifice for a supra-individual good. Suicide implies a rupture of human equilibrium and does violence to our fundamental instinct for life. Thus it is no exaggeration to see something neurotic in the desire or the attempt to commit suicide. Not all suicides are neurotic in the clinical sense of the word, but on the other hand there are neurotics in whom the temptation to suicide is a basic symptom of their condition. The principal characteristic of neurotic suicide is its apparent exemption from all objective motivation, or at least a flagrant disproportion between conscious motivation and the seriousness of the act.

One evening Maurice, a brilliant twenty-one-year-old student, stood in a Paris subway waiting for a train to take him to a friend's house. When the train emerged from the tunnel at high speed, a kind of vertigo overcame him and he threw himself on the rails. The conductor was able to stop the train in time and Maurice escaped with minor lacerations. This was not the first time he had attempted suicide. Once before he had jumped into the Seine; another time he took an overdose of sleeping pills. When he looks out the window of a high building, he is often tempted to leap. The doctor who treated him after the incident in the subway advised him to undergo psychotherapy. When he began treatment, Maurice could give no explanation of his suicidal tendencies. He was not unhappy in life; quite the contrary. He got along well with people and was in love with a charming girl. The future, far from filling him with fear, looked rosy. He was confident that he was talented enough to realize his ambitions, which were not at all modest. But, as he said, "It is stronger than I am." Without premeditation or conscious motivation, he has committed acts that would normally have killed him. Even his overwhelming fear of death could not restrain him. After a long analysis Maurice discovered the deeper causes of his compulsion to commit suicide. Of Jewish origin, he lost his parents in the Nazi camps while he was still an infant. For several years he lived in secrecy with some Christian friends of his parents. He was well treated but nothing could replace the parental love of which he had been so prematurely deprived. Because of this, his life instinct atrophied. Consciously he loved life, but to his unconscious it was full of dangers. This was what made death so irresistibly attractive to him. When therapy restored his confidence in life and removed his instinctual inhibitions, he was no longer tempted to suicide and was able to love and be loved.

When Olga, a pretty secretary of twenty-six, came to see me, she had just attempted her fourth suicide. Her parents were divorced and she had been brought up by her paternal grandmother, to whom she was extremely attached. "More attached than is normal," as she admitted herself. When her grandmother died, Olga lost interest in life and became bored to death. Love affairs provided temporary relief but, realizing that she was incapable of loving truly, she soon ended these affairs and reverted to her melancholy state. On three occasions she took heavy doses of sleeping pills. Did she really want to kill herself? She didn't know. Overcome with tedium, unable to sleep, and haunted by the memory of her happy childhood, she would suddenly, without any precise intent, empty the sleeping pills into a glass and consume them. She told herself that in death she would join her grandmother in the Hereafter. Olga lived in a dazed state, experiencing neither fear nor joy. Each time she took the pills she called a friend who managed to save her just in time. Her first three suicide attempts took place under similar circumstances. The last-minute arrival of a friend or neighbor always saved her life. The fourth and last time, she threw herself into the sea while she was vacationing in Corsica. A sailor rescued her. But Olga was as ungrateful to him as she had been to her other rescuers. She could not decide whether life was worth living or not. During the first months of therapy the danger of another attempt at suicide was always present. During the sessions she wept constantly and her conversation was dominated by the memory of her grandmother's life and sad death and her own boredom. Only after her infantile attachment to her grandmother had been resolved did Olga become interested in life and finally liberated from the temptation to suicide.

In my opinion, one should never recommend orthodox psychoanalysis to neurotics who are haunted by the fear of suicide. The neutrality and silence that are strictly required in an analyst would abandon the patient to his intolerable loneliness and boredom. This, added to the length of the treatment, is good reason to fear that the patient might commit suicide before he is cured. Only semidirective psychotherapy, where human contact between patient and therapist can be immediately established, is likely to help the patient live long enough to be cured.

Not all neurotics who are tempted by suicide are fortunate enough to benefit by therapy. After one or more attempts, many of them succeed in committing suicide, often against their own will. Neurotics rarely do anything for a positive motive. Most often, they give in to compulsions which they are unable to resist. The expression, "It is stronger than I am," is a recurrent one in their conversation. Those who fail in an attempted suicide can still seriously harm their health. Too, there are neurotics who practice indirect suicide by refusing, for example, to take care of themselves when they are sick, by eating improperly or abusing alcohol and narcotics. Such persons unconsciously want to destroy themselves. The relentless manner in which many people abuse themselves morally and socially can rightly be identified with the same refusal to live we have observed in actual suicides. But here again, there is no evidence for the existence of a "death instinct."

We often hear it said at cocktail parties that psychoanalysis is responsible for the suicide of someone known to one of the guests. The revelation in the course of analysis of such "horrors" as Oedipus complexes and incestuous tendencies, until now happily repressed, is said to have provoked such self-disgust that the patient was driven to suicide. In my various books, I have had occasion to criticize Freudians because their abusive use of certain terms can indeed traumatize the mentally ill. Intrafamilial attachments, for example, are rarely incestuous. The best Freudian psychologists, moreover, know this full well, but they claim that they give the word "incest" a meaning that it does not have in ordinary language. This "excuse" will scarcely do. To knowingly use words that are likely to traumatize a patient is irresponsible. Freud himself seems to have been more-or-less consciously motivated by the desire to scandalize the Viennese of his time, whom he despised and condemned as hypocrites. But on the whole, I am inclined to defend psychoanalysts against this charge. Neurotics who commit or attempt to commit suicide during analysis are few in number, proportionally far fewer than among those who do not receive psychological treatment. In the case of those who do attempt suicide, it seems the blame is to be laid less on analysis than upon the slowness of treatment, which may not liquidate the temptation to flee life quickly enough; but the temptation itself pre-existed treatment. In any case no experienced psychoanalyst, no matter what his theoretical position, would prematurely burden his patients with the "horrors" of the unconscious. It remains true, as I said earlier, that psychoanalytic jargon should be resolutely banned from the vocabulary of the practitioner while he is treating the sick. And when a suicidal tendency is detected, it is always preferable to replace psychoanalysis with a more active and rapid

method of psychotherapy, thus reducing or even preventing
the danger.

[4] BLACKMAIL AND SUICIDE

Jacqueline has always spread havoc around her. When she
was a little girl, before any conflict between her and her
mother had developed, she would threaten to kill herself.
Her mother was terrified and gave in constantly. Today Jacqueline is married and the mother of several children. She
threatens her own family in the same way. When a doctor
persuaded her to seek therapeutic treatment, she tried the
same tactic on the therapist whenever she thought he wasn't
agreeing with her. He did nothing to persuade her not to do
it; at the same time he naturally did not doubt her sincerity.
In due course it became clear that Jacqueline was quite sincere when she threatened to commit suicide. But her threats
were primarily, even though she was not altogether conscious
of this, an effective form of blackmail. The psychologist advised her husband not to attempt to stop her or doubt her
sincerity. When Jacqueline saw that her blackmail was no
longer working, she gave it up.

A relatively large number of people, particularly neurotic
or depressed women, threaten to commit suicide. Many of
them, like Jacqueline, practice blackmail on their families.
And like her, they are as a rule not aware of the ambiguity
of their motives. They are sincerely convinced that their lives
are intolerable, that their relatives do not understand them.
They almost always exhibit paranoic tendencies. A girl of
seventeen jumped from a seventh-story window simply because her mother wouldn't let her go dancing. But such

actions are extremely rare among people who frequently
threaten to commit suicide. When they do execute their
threats they almost always succeed in taking one pill less
than the fatal dosage, hanging themselves with a rope that
is just a little too fragile, or shooting themselves a little to
one side of a vital organ. In most cases there is no question
of conscious calculation; their life instincts unconsciously
protect them. When this kind of "blackmail" threat is successfully carried out, it is generally by accident. Even the
young lady who jumped from the seventh-story window was
probably the victim of her erroneous unconscious intent.
She had threatened to jump many times before, but her
parents had either yielded to her demands or restrained her
by force. This time the mother arrived a minute too late to
prevent her taking the fatal step.

Most people who threaten suicide to blackmail others have
no intention of carrying out their threats unless their bluff is
called. Mrs. N. contemplated suicide during periods of depression, but her son's solicitude would prevent her from taking action. When she recovered she would continue to mention her desire to commit suicide in a possessive effort to
keep her son in the same state of affectionate dependence as
during her illness. She particularly insisted that he spend all
of his free evenings with her. One night when he wanted to
go out with his fiancée Mrs. N. spoke in a melancholy way
of suicide. He begged her on bended knees to give up such
foolish thoughts. Then, trusting in the power of prayer, he
went out. As soon as he left she turned on the gas. Very
likely she would not have done so had her son taken a firmer
stand. His obsequious attitude convinced her of the dramatic
"grandeur" of her gesture, and possessive mothers often show
a taste for the dramatic.

We should never let people practicing this sort of blackmail know that we are on to their game. They want desperately to be taken seriously. If we make fun of them they will feel obliged to carry out their threats, whereas at bottom they aren't really serious about it. In their desire to appear "consistent," they feel they must risk the deed even against their will. Awkward interventions on the part of members of the family or friends also have little chance of success. Mrs. S., who had taken an overdose of barbiturates, was saved from death by the rapid arrival of a doctor. When she recovered, she blamed her husband for her attempted suicide and accused him of wanting to assassinate her. But her husband had done nothing more than laugh ironically when she threatened to take her life after a mild family squabble. It was out of pity for herself and in anger against her husband that she took the barbiturates.

Those whose difficult lot it is to live with people having suicidal tendencies should restrict themselves to discreet supervision. They are in the grip of rather serious neurotic conflicts and the best service we can render is to convince them to undergo psychotherapy or analysis. They have to be cured less of their desire to commit suicide than of their often unconscious desire to practice blackmail, which is generally a raw form of the will to dominate others.

[5] ROMANTIC SUICIDE

Some "romantic" suicides could also be called "metaphysical." This type of suicide was very much in fashion at certain periods of history and flourished particularly in the years following World War I. Young intellectuals, or those who thought they were, tried to imitate Novalis or

Baudelaire by affecting a contempt for life. They hoped to reach the summit of freedom and self-exaltation by killing themselves "for nothing," i.e., for no objective reason but merely because they had had enough of life or they wanted to experience death. Not so long ago, they pretended to be inspired by Gide's concept of the "gratuitous act" and later the "absurdism" of Camus.

Most of those who commit suicide for love belong to the "romantic" category. They kill themselves because a loved one does not share their feelings or because love's path is strewn with obstacles that are apparently insurmountable or because they consider love too exalted and too pure to be exposed to the inevitable profanations of life. We will discuss the relationship between death and love in the following chapter. Here we shall analyze romantic suicide, whether motivated by love or by "metaphysics."

At the age of seventeen, George fell madly in love with an older cousin. He wrote passionate letters and poetry to her, but she refused to take his adolescent passion seriously and joked in the company of friends about what she took to be a childish game. Moreover, George did not expect his love to be reciprocated. He judged himself absolutely unworthy of his cousin's love. Drawing inspiration from romantic literature, he took great satisfaction in playing the role of the unhappy lover. He would tell his friends that he considered all happy love banal. During vacations by the seashore he would follow his cousin about, heaving sighs of distress, but at a safe distance and taking pains not to be seen by her. One day he spied her flirting with another man. This was too much for George. He felt betrayed, ran to the house, wrote a letter of explanation to his cousin, seized his father's revolver and shot himself in the chest. Happily no vital organ was affected. After a few weeks in the hospital George was cured of his wound, his love, and probably of romanticism for ever. Unfortunately, not all romantics are so lucky.

Sometimes a double suicide is the result of a love affair. Such was the case with Elaine and Bernard. Her parents were opposed to her marrying Bernard because they did not think he was "good" enough for their daughter. The two lovers fled to the Riviera, spent all their money in a night club, made love and immediately afterwards drove their automobile over a cliff. In other cases, the man kills his companion and then takes his own life. But not infrequently, when his moment of truth comes, he lacks the courage to follow his beloved in death. Then he generally simulates suicide in the hope that he will look good in the eyes of his parents and the judges. This is what happened to Peter. No one objected to his love for Sophia, but an "ordinary" love wasn't enough for a young man who had read widely in Novalis and other romantic poets. He wanted his love to be absolutely pure. A good talker, he had little difficulty convincing Sophia that they should consummate their sublime love with a "beautiful death." They retired to a "romantic" forest and, after reading poetry and exchanging chaste kisses, Peter killed Sophia with a revolver. But when he turned the weapon on himself his hand trembled with fear and he only wounded himself slightly. Before the judges, he played, not without sincerity, the role of one who regretted that he had not followed his beloved into the "kingdom of shadows." Deep inside, he was glad that he had escaped death, although he did not seem to be particularly sorry that he had killed the girl.

Romantic suicide is almost always committed by men. And in all double suicides that I am familiar with, the man has always taken the initiative. I know of no case where, once the couple decided to die together, the woman first killed her lover and then committed suicide. Women, of course, commit suicide "for love" but almost always because they are abandoned or deceived by the man they loved. This kind of suicide can scarcely be called "romantic". A woman who loves and knows she is loved never thinks of death. The most miserable life with her loved one would be preferable. We may conclude that woman is, by reason of her psychological make-up, too realistic to be tempted by the game of romanticism. For, however tragic the deaths of some romantics may be, we cannot help suspecting that they were playing a game and were hoisted with their own petard. We know that children take their games very seriously. Romantics, although of adult age, remain children in many important psychological ways. Thus they generally take their dangerous games with death seriously. I have talked to a number of women who escaped "romantic suicides." Not one confessed to having wanted to die. But their lovers convinced them that only death could prove the sublimity of love and they dared not show themselves less generous for fear that the authenticity of their love would be suspect. Thus they consented to die.

As I noted earlier, love is not the only reason for romantic suicide. Oscar, nineteen years old, was in love with nobody. His family was comfortably well-to-do, and he had everything he wanted. But Oscar over-identified with the heros of romantic literature. He judged the "crass materialism" of his family and society mercilessly. In his clothes and style of life he tried to distinguish himself as much as possible from his surroundings. Naturally he felt misunderstood by his family. The life they offered him seemed insipid. But instead of trying to modify his situation according to his aspirations, he preferred to die. And so he committed suicide.

In Oscar's case, as in those of many other romantic suicides, the psychologist easily detects paranoic symptoms. These people consider themselves too exceptional to be understood. At bottom, they feel that life is unworthy of them.

[6] MYSTICAL SUICIDES

This category, from a psychological point of view, resembles romantic suicide. But there is this difference: while the romantic commits suicide in the name of his own ego, the mystic dies for what he takes to be a transcendent cause.

Some decades ago a preacher—half charlatan, half mystic —in a mountain village of Germany succeeded in creating such a climate of religious exaltation that all the inhabitants, animated by the desire to be united with Christ as soon as possible in heaven, hanged themselves from trees. And this is not a unique case. In many countries, at different times and within different religious groups, similar episodes have transpired. In an ambiance of collective delirium, during religious festivals for example, a number of people may suddenly take their own lives. Death in such cases is the crowning of ecstacy. Certain "old believers" in Russia, rather than renounce their archaic practices which had been condemned by the official church, sometimes had recourse to collective suicide by fire. This was also the case with certain eccentric sects of the Middle Ages. And more recently, Spanish anarchists committed suicide to the cry of "Long live my death!"

Mystical suicide is not always collective. Thus the Buddhists in Vietnam burn themselves to death to show their disagreement with a political policy or the war that the Americans are waging in their country. Mystical suicides of this kind customarily spread like contagious disease. One Buddhist monk after another offers himself as a holocaust. Their example has been imitated in the United States. All involved were convinced of the transcendent import of their suicides and their influence upon the affairs of the world. This type of suicide, from a psychological point of view, must be considered sacrificial.

Mystical suicide clearly cannot be explained as cowardice. It is motivated by the conviction that this life is not the whole life, that it is far from constituting the supreme good for man. But there are times when we have the distinct impression that the individuals involved are temporarily deranged, that they are not acting rationally, so much so that we can with justification speak of "mystical madness."

Mystics who have the power of inducing their followers to commit suicide are not necessarily religious. It seems that some Germans, frenzied by Nazi propaganda, worked themselves into a state that was subjectively quite similar to those of the Buddhist monks or the old Russian Christians. They killed themselves with the same fervor that they turned on others when enjoined to do so by their leaders. They, too, set a higher price upon certain collective values than on their individual lives.

It is also obvious that neurotic factors play an important role in many mystical suicides. Furthermore, scholars have shown that it is not always easy to distinguish between true and false mysticism, and even genuine mystics are not always exempt from neurotic disturbances.

[7] A TENTATIVE PSYCHOLOGICAL EXPLANATION

What do these different suicidal types have in common? Freud, always faithful to some of the basic postulates of his own theories, thought that suicide was caused by aggressiveness. Normally this is directed towards another; failing this, it is turned on the subject himself. Stekel, once Freud's friend and later the founder of his own school of depth psychology, argued that suicide was motivated by a desire for the abyss or a return to the maternal womb. Thus those who commit suicide are infantile, incapable of confronting the demands of life. Other psychologists have proposed different explanations consistent with their general theories of the psychic life and neurosis.

It must be admitted that the task of the psychologist who tries to link all types of suicide to a single motive is not an easy one. Evidence indicates that, from a psychological point of view, there is a great difference between those who commit suicide because life is too much for them and those who do so for romantic reasons. Those who kill themselves in states of neurotic depression or mystical ecstasy represent still another category. The divisions we have proposed, however, are not rigid. The same person can be both a neurotic and a coward, a romantic and a mystic. Each suicidal type, like any other human being, is a singular and complex reality. Our classifications are more didactic than anything else; they are intended to help us understand the problem. When a psychologist is dealing with someone who has tried to commit suicide or manifests a desire to do so, he forgets his categories and becomes interested in the individual as someone unique. His experience with other suicidal types can certainly be useful to him but it should not induce him to make hasty generalizations.

Thus warned against generalizations and dogmatism, we may now turn to an investigation of the traits common to all suicides or at least a majority of them. On the basis of my own experience, I would say that most suicidal types share a common sense of life's valuelessness. Depending on the case, this sense can be more or less conscious but, except in cases of sudden madness, it seems to be a universal trait of those who attempt suicide. In some men, the life instinct is so imperious that nothing daunts them. They would accept the most humiliating disgrace or the most intense suffering in order to continue living. But in those with suicidal tendencies this instinct is, at least temporarily, inhibited. Thus they are defeated by difficulties and obstacles that they could normally surmount. We cannot but be astonished at the futility of the motives most men give for their desire to commit suicide.

Yet these men are just as afraid of death as others. Some of them are absolutely terrified of it. But they are even more afraid of the trials and responsibilities of life.

However, not all who commit suicide are cowards. Seneca, Marcus Aurelius, Cato and Hannibal (to mention but a few well known personalities who took their own lives) all gave ample proof of their courage in life. But even they made no secret of their contempt, or at least indifference, for life. Like the Stoics, they believed that it has no meaning in itself; it is no more than a theatrical play. For them, to commit suicide amounted to no more than leaving the theatre because the play was boring or otherwise unsatisfactory. Since life was held to have no intrinsic meaning or purpose, nothing obliged the individual to live longer than he wanted to.

The Stoic tradition has always encouraged the most radical individualism. It teaches that man's dignity consists in his independence from all external influences. This is the golden rule of Stoicism. Nothing prohibits man from taking his own life when he tires of it. The Stoic Celsus criticized the Christian martyrs, not because they preferred death to life, but rather because they based their choice on love for a non-existent God rather than on cold reason.

Kirilov, Dostoevsky's celebrated hero, killed himself to prove man's absolute freedom. He, too, was in the Stoic tradition, but with the difference that there was a good deal of passion in his rebellion against God and none of the serenity so much prized by the Stoics. Kirilov's philosophy, more than that of the Stoics, seems to underlie the literary work of André Malraux and Albert Camus. Their heroes rebel against God and society with the deliberate intention of liberating themselves from the absurdity and fatality of human destiny. The hope of substituting a new order for the present disorder and injustice does not seem to have seriously concerned them, and for this reason they are more rebels than revolutionaries. The only thing that restrained Camus from coming out categorically in favor of suicide was the fear that he would thereby become the accomplice of an absurd destiny. "To cease voluntarily to live," he wrote, "would be to play death's game. Suicide would extinguish the flame of revolt." In the end, Camus preferred to be a victim rather than an accomplice of destiny.

Is Stocism genuinely alive today? Many invoke the principles of that tradition but few seem to practice them. Among the many suicide cases I have known, either directly or indirectly by posthumous letters, not one was as serene in the face of death as, for example, Seneca.

We have distinguished the neurotic type of suicide from other categories. This means that in the former category, neurotic influences are particularly evident while in other categories the psychologist can discover objective and conscious motives. In fact, almost all who commit suicide exhibit schizoid tendencies. All have broken or lost the sense of those vital values that bind men to one another, the world and history. In this sense we may say that the suicide is dead long before he kills himself. As we pointed out in our first chapter, death is above all a radical separation from others, from the whole human community.

Neurosis, according to Freud, is the result of the eruption into consciousness of a powerful repressed instinct. Orthodox psychoanalysis concentrated primarily on the damage caused by the repression of the sexual instinct, the libido. But infinitely more powerful than this is the life instinct, of which the sex urge is in reality a sub-instinct. Repression of the sexual instinct is, to be sure, capable of causing trouble, but it rarely affects the core of the personality. When the life instinct is repressed, on the other hand, suicide seems a logical course of action. Whether death is faced with Stoical serenity or motivated by cowardice and depression, suicide is in all cases caused by a life instinct that has ceased to function normally.

This is even true of Buddhist monks who indulge in particularly horrible forms of suicide. They are not, strictly speaking, motivated by courage. The principal purpose of the asceticism they practice is precisely the extinction of the will to live, i.e., the life instinct.

From a technical point of view, the life instinct is not dead as long as there is life. In any case, we have been speaking of the inhibition or repression of the life instinct rather than its extinction. Modern depth psychology has perfected the techniques of abolishing inhibitions and liberating what has been repressed. Thus, suicide is never necessary even for one obsessed by the idea. There can obviously be no question of "reasoning" with someone who is thinking about suicide. Any experienced psychologist knows that it is not effective therapy to deal only with the symptoms of a mental illness. To do so would be to tilt at windmills. Psychotherapy must try to cure the schizoid or paranoic tendencies in the patient, and re-establish the framework of his emotional relationships to other men and the universe at large. Gradually, in the course of treatment, the life instinct will revive and the will to live be reborn. We cited earlier the case of Olga, who had made four attempts to commit suicide, and for evidently neurotic motives. After beginning treatment, she was never tempted again. Toward the end of her therapy she said with some surprise, "When I think that only a few months ago I so desperately wanted to die! Now it seems that no matter what happens to me I will never think of taking my own life." And yet the explanation of this metamorphosis is very simple. Whereas previously Olga was turned in upon herself, she now feels herself to be a fully integral part of the world around her. When she walks in the forest she now sees trees, flowers and birds whereas before she was indifferent to such things.

[8] THE RIGHT TO SUICIDE?

I am speaking in this book as a psychologist rather than a moralist. But some readers may have the impression that I consider suicide a moral evil as well as a disease to be treated by medical science. The laws of many countries in fact condemn suicide as a crime.

Individualistic moralists and philosophers do not object in principle to a person's intention to commit suicide. Since everyone lives for himself and is the master of his own life, nothing is more logical than the right to renounce that life when the individual so pleases. We have already spoken at length of the Stoic respect for suicide. Closer to our own times, Montaigne looked upon suicide as "the pleasure of affirming one's independence from nature by taking its place. . . . The most voluntary death is the most beautiful. Our life depends on the will of others; death can depend on our own will." According to Henri de Montherlant, also a great admirer of the Stoics, suicide in addition procures the superior man "the pleasure of withdrawing from the lot of the common man," who docilely submits to the law of nature. And Dostoevsky's Kirilov exclaimed, "Whoever wants supreme freedom must kill himself. He who dares to take his own life is God!"

Perhaps Christianity's fundamental anti-individualism is nowhere more manifest than in its categorical rejection of a man's right to take his own life. Almost all moralists outside of Christianity are at least tolerant with respect to suicide and often admire it. The Christian believes that life is a gift of God over which man has no proprietary rights. He is a mere depository. Christian morality admits no distinction between murder and suicide. In both cases man is infringing upon God's rights. In practice, the Church is far more lenient toward murder, many forms of which she justifies, than toward suicide. Moreover, statistics show that suicide is more prevalent in Protestant countries than in Catholic ones. The reason for this is not only that Catholicism is especially categorical in its condemnation of suicide and refuses to grant it that "romantic" admiration it often enjoys elsewhere but, more importantly, that the Catholic doctrine of the mystical body reinforces the natural social bond among men and thus rejects individualism more resolutely.

St. Thomas Aquinas based his rejection of suicide on the natural law, in much the same spirit as he tried to prove the perfect conformity of all Christian morality with the natural law. Like Aristotle, he begins with the principle that man does not belong to himself but to society, being by definition a "social animal." Suicide is a crime of homicide against society, depriving it of one of its members just as surely as if one had murdered his neighbor. On this point, Marxist morality is in perfect accord with Thomism. It does admit the legitimacy of suicide in the alienated world of capitalism, but absolutely nothing could justify it in the reconciled world of socialism. It is well known that the press in communist countries refuses to publish statistics on the number of suicides committed. A young Russian poet, taking advantage of the relative freedom that followed de-Stalinization, created something of a scandal by recalling that two of the most renowned poets of the revolution, Iessenine and Maïakovsky, committed suicide because they found the Communist regime intolerable. But St. Thomas does not argue that suicide is a crime in the name of social utilitarianism, but rather because it implies a violation of the duty of charity which every man has to himself as a creation of God.

It is important, however, to bear in mind that the problem of man's right to commit suicide has not always been construed in such simple terms, even by Christians. Thus Paul Landsberg, a German Catholic philosopher who was killed by the Nazis in 1944, confessed that he was psychologically and philosophically disposed to consider suicide justified in certain extreme circumstances. Living in constant danger of being betrayed to the authorities and realizing that he lacked the heroic character necessary to suffer sophisticated Nazi torture courageously, he carried a lethal poison on his person until 1942. "I think the idea of suicide," he wrote, "is less an expression of despair than of hope, although perhaps mad and perverted, addressed to the great unknown region of the hereafter." We learned later, however, that before Landsberg was arrested and died of exhaustion in a concentration camp at Orianenburg, he had renounced this position and destroyed the poison he had so long and in so many dangerous escapades carried on his person. On the other hand, he does not seem to have changed his philosophical opinion on the subject of suicide. The letters he wrote to friends in the last period of his life attest to his rapid development as a mystic. In his posthumous book, *The Moral Problem of Suicide,* Landsberg writes that the only argument against the right to commit suicide seems to him the duty every Christian has to imitate Christ. All arguments against suicide from natural law fail to stand up to critical examination and in any case are unconvincing in the eyes of a man who is sufficiently motivated psychologically to do away with a life that has grown intolerable. I agree with this position. Paul Landsberg in fact underwent a cruel death because of his conviction. He had been much impressed by St. Peter's admonition: "We must not, brethren, feel suffering for Christ, since he freely gave himself up to death for our salvation." At first, Landsberg was impressed by the last part of the sentence, which seemed to him to justify the kind of suicide that is motivated, not by boredom with life, but by the courage to die voluntarily. But later, after his own spiritual outlook had matured, he saw in it an exhortation to imitate Christ. Since Christ had willingly submitted to violent death, Landsberg concluded that the Christian can imitate Christ by permitting himself to be killed by persecutors although not by killing himself.

Another philosopher of great spiritual insight, Louis Lavelle, found the idea of suicide repulsive. Since life is sacred, suicide is a "sacred crime." "The fact that one man refuses to live," he wrote, "seems to condemn all life." In my opinion, Lavelle is too severe in his judgment of suicide. It would be correct if men committed suicide in all liberty and lucidity. But we have seen that only the exceptional Stoics manage to take their lives with such a heightened awareness of what they are doing. In all other cases, the deep psychological motives for such a decision are the result of a serious inhibition of the life instinct or a crippling neurosis. Suicide represents a choice that is more or less determined.

If we could abstract from each suicide its subjective motives, I would be inclined to agree with Lavelle and Christian moralists in their categorical rejection of suicide. Whatever form it takes and under whatever conditions it happens, suicide is always an act of absolute separation from the universe and other members of the human community, a violent rupture of those relationships that are the very foundation of the human condition. He who commits suicide not only kills himself but in fact injures all life, since by his action he deprives it of his assistance. Thus, objectively, he rejects human and cosmic solidarity. Those who die naturally or accidently also deprive the community of their help and are equally separated from it. But they have no moral responsibility for their fate. This is the principal theoretical difference between natural death and suicide—and I consider accidental "natural" in this perspective. All death is sorrowful but suicide is tragic.

It is one thing to condemn suicide and another to judge him who commits suicide. Unlike the philosopher or theologian, the psychologist is more concerned with the victim. Even the Catholic Church takes into consideration the many subjective factors which lead men and women to commit acts which are in themselves criminal. Thus in principle the Church refuses Christian burial to those who take their own lives yet in practice grants it frequently. This inconsistency is generally justified by the victim's "mental aberration," an expression that covers a number of quite different realities. It formerly meant insanity as such but today can refer to such states as depression and despair.

It seems, then, that we might offer a reasonably exact synthesis of contemporary theological, moral, sociological and psychological positions in the following manner: Suicide as such is reprehensible but we must have a great deal of understanding of and pity for the victims of suicide. The problem of suicide calls not so much for moral condemnation as for a battle against the principal causes of suicide, in particular against neurosis, loneliness and depression. The problem is, in fact, far more psychological than either sociological or moral.

[9]   VOLUNTARY DEATH

A clear distinction must be made between suicide, which we have just been analyzing, and *voluntary death*. Suicide appears to be a form of death that is freely chosen except perhaps in the case of certain neurotics who don't realize what they are doing. What we here refer to as voluntary death is *materially* the same as suicide. However, there is a great difference between the two from the point of view of intention.

During the German occupation a French resistant whom we shall call Pierre fell into the hands of the Gestapo. He had been an important figure in the underground and the Germans tortured him mercilessly in an effort to make him talk. Pierre resisted courageously, but he was growing weak and feared that he would not be able to hold out much longer. When the guards were momentarily distracted he jumped out the window and killed himself on the pavement below. Many other resistants would have done likewise in similar circumstances, preferring to die rather than betray the cause for which they had fought. Such men are not cowards; their life instinct is not repressed, nor are they romantics or neurotics. We are dealing here with charity, a sacrificial consent to death. Men like Pierre do not consider their individual lives the supreme good. Nor would they be refused a religious burial. On the contrary they are frequently compared to martyrs in sermons, and held up as examples for the young. Thomas Aquinas, who was so resolutely opposed to suicide, wrote: "To deliver oneself to death for a friend is one of the most virtuous of acts." How much more virtuous must it be to voluntarily sacrifice oneself for a noble cause or for a great number of men.

A soldier who goes on a mission so dangerous that there is little chance for him to return alive is in the above category, even though he did not volunteer for the mission. The code of the sea used to call for the captain to go down with his ship. More recently, a Catholic priest imprisoned in Dachau offered to take the place of a Jewish father of a family who had been condemned to death. His death was obviously voluntary. Socrates died voluntarily in the sense that he refused to let his friends save him. And Christ, knowing that "his hour had come," did nothing to avoid the suffering and death that awaited him. Those who most severely condemn suicide nonetheless admire those who freely accept death. The followers of Christ have always considered his voluntary death the supreme proof of his love for men.

The distinction between suicide and voluntary death is by no means arbitrary. However attentuated the moral responsibility of those who commit suicide and however great our compassion for them, it remains a fact that their motives are almost always egocentric and negative, since they renounce their relationship to the universe and the human community. But generosity and self-sacrifice characterize those who die voluntarily. Far from denying the universe and the human community, they willingly die for them.

But a qualification is in order. To justify and admire someone who submits to voluntary death we must take into consideration the cause for which he dies as well as his state of mind. First of all, we do not have the right to sacrifice our life except for a serious cause. Thus we cannot approve of the former custom of dueling, since the reasons for it were generally inconsequential. To have suffered an insult, personal or otherwise, in no way justifies the taking of a life. What was called "honor" in those times was often nothing more than wounded vanity.

The cause for which one dies must also be objectively worthwhile. Young Nazis in Hitler's Germany readily gave up their lives. They enthusiastically volunteered for the most dangerous missions and maneuvers. Subjectively, their spirit of sacrifice was as praiseworthy as that of the resistants in conquered countries. But the two groups must be judged by a different moral standard because the moral value of the causes they died for were not at all the same.

IV

Death and Love

*A pleasure stronger than
death.*
—ST. AUGUSTINE

ONE evening I arrived late at a lecture given by an
American Negro psychiatrist. He was speaking in French and
often used a word that sounded like *"lamor."* I thought he
was talking about death. Since many of his ideas struck me
as strange I asked him to clarify some points. He then informed the audience that he was speaking of *amour* and not
mort. Like many of his compatriots he pronounced the
French "ou" like an "o." What is interesting about this little
story is that it took about fifteen minutes for everyone to
understand that the speaker was talking about love rather
than death. Are the two so closely associated in the unconscious?

We might recall in this context the connection Freud postu-
lated between love, which he reduced to libido, and death.
In his view the death instinct was the most fundamental of
all man's impulses, and the libido itself, in the final analysis,

served the cause of death. We have already contested this hypothesis at some length. Nonetheless, it seems to be the case, from the point of view of depth psychology, that a dialectical struggle takes place between the forces of love and the forces of death.

[I] ROMANTIC DEATH

As a system of thought and a literary school, Romanticism was a phenomenon of the nineteenth century. But as an attitude of mind, a psychological stance, it has always existed and is still with us today. On the question of the relationship between love and death, for example, the attitude of medieval chivalry was typically "romantic." Before going off to war or engaging in a duel, the knights always claimed to be risking death for their loved ones. Today there are many people who pride themselves on seeing in love no more than a biological reality, stripped of all romanticism and disassociated from death. But we have only to look about us to see that there is as much romanticism today as ever before, particularly among the young.

The literature and folklore of all peoples in every age deal with the mysterious relationship between death and love. All "romantic" literature testifies that man can and sometimes must die for love. We have already spoken of suicide motivated by love. Romanticism does not see in such suicide the defeat of love and the triumph of death. On the contrary, death is believed to serve the cause of love; it removes all obstacles from love's path and makes eternal what otherwise would only be contingent. Romantic lovers often find it difficult to be together, perhaps because one of them is already married or their parents oppose their union or for some other reason. But death dissolves the marriage bond and puts the lovers beyond the pale of parental control. Even the Christian ages, so severe in the judgment of suicide, looked indulgently upon those who voluntarily died for love. And the same is true in our own positivistic and materialistic age.

Romantic death for love is not always violent, nor do the lovers always take their own lives. Tristan and Isolde did not commit suicide. Death mercifully delivered them from a life in which their love could not be consummated. Since they were prevented from loving one another on earth they desired death and their wish was granted. Death not only delivered them from the torments of separation from one another but also justified their love. While alive, they were merely another adulterous couple, but death sanctified their love and for centuries they have been considered ideal lovers.

It is easy to understand how the legend of Tristan and Isolde could have inspired the romantic Richard Wagner. Strongly influenced by the pessimistic philosophy of Schopenhauer, Wagner spoke of the death of Tristan and Isolde as a dissolution in the One, death's victory over love. "The night of love gives eternal oblivion. To become one with the breath of the world is the supreme pleasure." Freudians see in these words the subordination of love to the death instinct, but Wagner's sensibility was too authentically romantic to be contained by Schopenhauer's pessimistic vision. Lovers do not aspire to nothingness in dying but rather to the fulfillment of their love in an eternal and most intimate fusion of hearts.

External circumstances and the will of others are not the only obstacles to the perfect fulfillment of romantic love. The lovers also come up against all the insurmountable obstacles of their own imperfections. All orgasms and ecstasies are followed by relapse into commonplace routine. Romantics rely on death to put an end to banalities and render love pure and eternal.

In real life there is no love like that of Tristan and Isolde. Yet poets continue to be fascinated by the theme. Although not inspired by romantic sources, Paul Claudel, that great singer of passionate love, establishes a close connection between death and love in various of his plays. Only in death does Prouhèze finally possess Rodrigue (*The Annunciation Made to Mary*). Violeine's love for Jacques makes her death inevitable (*The Satin Slipper*). Death is also the outcome of the love between Mésa and Ysé (*Le Partage du Midi*). Depending on the version of the legend, Tristan and Isolde die sometimes of sorrow, sometimes of joy. For Claudel, death for love is always tragic; it takes on the characteristics of a sacrifice. The three men she loves cause Ysé's death. Violeine and Prouhèze died so that Jacques and Rodigue, whom they love, can fully realize their destiny.

There are elements of hope and despair in romantic death. Ysé rejoices because death intervenes before her youth and beauty have faded. She hopes that death will fix her youth and beauty in the soul of her lover forever.

In the nineteenth century, death from consumption was frequent, as may be recalled from *The Lady of the Camellias*, *La Traviata* and many other novels and operas. But neither Dumas nor Verdi had to draw their themes from legend; daily life supplied them in abundance. While Tristan and Isolde, as well as Claudel's heroines, sought in death the consummation of love which life refused them, nineteenth-century heroes died because they were unhappy in love. In view of the insights provided by modern psychology, it is not surprising that this kind of death was considered romantic and mysterious. In all psychosomatic diseases, emotional conflicts play a determining role. One who loves without being loved in return loses interest in life; a life without love seems empty and not worth living. The romantic conception of love encouraged this kind of unhappiness. It conceived of love as a difficult and rare thing. It was generally held that there could be only one "true love" in a lifetime. Furthermore, it is characteristic of all passionate lovers to think of themselves as absolutely unique. Consequently, they take themselves very seriously. Men and women of this period were only too inclined to take any and all amorous passions for "great loves." If the object of such passion did not respond in a similar fashion, the rejected one could only feel condemned to eternal unhappiness. To lack this feeling would have depreciated the lover's passion in his own eyes and those of observers. Under such conditions, interest in life naturally diminished, thus preparing the way for sickness and death. Moreover, such languorous lovers rarely took care of themselves and considered their enfeebled state to be proof of the authenticity of their passion. They hoped thus to impress others, particularly their beloved, with the depth of their love and how wronged they had been.

The most common love-sickness was, unsurprisingly, tuberculosis. Together with stomach ulcers and other maladies of the digestive system, tuberculosis is undoubtedly one of the illnesses most frequently caused by emotional conflicts. But stomach disorders are rarely lethal, while in the nineteenth century consumption always killed. Moreover, there is nothing romantic about stomach diseases. No one would dare say, "I have a stomachache because I am unhappy in love." But tuberculosis was the disease *par excellence;* a languishing romantic could be proud to have it and proud to die of it.

In the romantic perspective, one could die of too much

love as well as too little. I do not know whether anyone ever died *naturally* because of an excess of joy. But the theme is a recurrent one in romantic poetry. Young lovers frequently committed suicide when they thought they had reached the paroxysm of happiness. They feared that with time their love would fade and lose its romantic beauty. Innumerable lovers have whispered these words of Baudelaire to one another: "Let us love and die together."

Today we have a far less romantic attitude toward love. Not many people think they are limited to one love in a lifetime. Our problem is rather that we don't take love seriously enough, and love and being in love are often confused. It is human to suffer when one's love is not reciprocated, and lovers are just as jealous of rivals as they were in the Romantic Age. Moreover, fashion plays an important role in our attitudes toward love. The great Romantic poets—Nerval, Novalis, and others—reflected their times, but they also contributed to shaping the ideas and feelings of their age. The same is true today. Young people who have been influenced by the novels of Françoise Sagan, for instance, do not take love seriously enough for death to be a threat to it.

Still, although rare, Romanticism is not altogether dead. I know of at least two cases that bear tragic testimony to its survival. And I am speaking here only of nonviolent death directly caused by love.

Charles, thirty years old, fell hopelessly in love with Gisele, his best friend's wife. This was not his first affair, but he felt that it was his first "true" love. He wrote poetic and passionate letters to Gisele. He did not have seduction in mind; in fact he did not expect that his letters would be answered. Gisele was at first surprised, then flattered that she was able to arouse such passion in a man of such substantial intellectual and moral qualities. But she was incapable of such passion and furthermore got on well with her husband. Still, she wanted to appease Charles' torments of love and show him that she was by no means insensitive to his attentions. So she decided to become his mistress. She entered this relationship with the air of an experienced woman who naturally achieves her ends. But this was not what Charles wanted. He felt terribly guilty toward Gisele's husband and believed that his great love had been irremediably profaned. For several days he remained in a severe state of anxiety. Then he suffered an attack of asthma and died before a doctor could reach him. We might note that Charles had had asthma when he was an adolescent, but he had responded to medical treatment and had not had an attack for fourteen years. It seems, indeed, that love brought about the final attack.

The other case I am familiar with concerns Catherine, a twenty-six-year-old schoolteacher. For years she had been in love with her sister's husband. The latter, not unaware of the young woman's feelings, became her lover. The idyll lasted seven years and was attended by all the torments of conscience and complications of clandestinity that are inseparable from this kind of love. Finally he grew tired of her, became interested in other women and one day abruptly informed her that their affair was over. In her inexperience, Catherine had not noticed the change that had been gradually taking place in her lover. The sudden realization that she had been betrayed and abandoned deprived her of all interest in life. She stopped eating and in a matter of weeks had lost over twenty pounds. When her friends finally persuaded her to see a doctor, it was too late; she was hospitalized with tuberculosis and died shortly afterwards. Since she had no desire to be cured, all medical treatment was ineffective.

We might point out that in both of the above cases death ended an unhappy and guilty love. I don't think that men today are very inclined to die of happy love.

[2] CRIMES OF LOVE

To die of love, like Charles and Catherine, is rare today. But love continues to sow the seeds of death, although generally independently of any Romantic association. There is still many a Thérèse Desquéroux [a character in François Mauriac's novel *Thérèse*] among us, particularly in the country, women who patiently and systematically plot their husband's deaths. Having ceased to love them, they want to be rid of them and marry other men. Men, and some women, are less patient. Circuit courts in provincial cities deal with crimes of love every year. X arranged an automobile accident to do away with his wife because she stood in the way of his union with another woman. Y killed her husband in the hope, generally fallacious, that the crime would be blamed on a hunting accident or an armed robber. That intelligent men and women can be blinded by passionate love is proven by the naive way in which such crimes are usually executed. One does not have to be a Sherlock Holmes or Inspector Maigret to immediately detect their amateur character. It is surprising, given the fact that so few crimes of this nature succeed, that so many people still commit them. We might also note that crimes of love are not always committed solely for love. There are often sordid material motives as well. When a farmer's wife kills her husband out of love for a young farm hand, it often turns out that the latter had coveted the farm more than the woman.

Many crimes of love are motivated by jealousy, but it

would be wrong to see in jealousy a criterion of the authenticity of love. Wounded vanity, rather than love, is generally the reason for such crimes.

When Hubert learned that his wife was deceiving him, he planned a most terrible death for both his wife and her lover. Concealing himself in the apartment, he waited until the lovers had gone to sleep. He then poured gasoline on the bed and ignited it. He was aware of the risk he ran and didn't even take the trouble to concoct an alibi. The irony of this case is that Hubert had ceased to love his wife and had left her for another woman. But as soon as he learned that she was seeing another man and seemed to be happy with him he was overcome by an intolerable jealousy. He resolved upon revenge at any price, regardless of the consequences. Jealous types of this sort are psychologically very much like possessive children who would rather destroy a toy they are no longer interested in than give it to someone else.

The story of a particularly horrible crime of jealousy was recently reported in the newspapers. A young woman with two infant sons left her husband because he drank, openly deceived her with other women and beat her. Despite his supplications, she refused to come back to him. Furious, he hid in the woods near a river where he knew his wife often took the children for walks. When the opportunity presented itself he seized the children and drowned them, the prayers and promises of their mother notwithstanding. This man was, on the testimony of his neighbors and even his wife, very fond of his children. Jealousy, however, was stronger than his other feelings and compelled him to seek revenge.

The love that underlies crimes of jealousy is a possessive love for the other as object and sometimes takes the form of a perverted love of self.

Juries are generally indulgent toward crimes of love. Acquittal is frequent, especially in cases where the wife kills an unfaithful husband. Men, who comprise most juries, still find their "intellectual" nourishment in novels that make much of the irresistible force of passion in general and of jealousy in particular. As a result murders that in reality are the most abject of criminal acts often masquerade as crimes of love.

I do not share this popular partiality towards crimes of love. No experienced psychologist can ignore the radical conflict between love and the desire to kill, whether the object of aggression be another or one's self. Authentic love always serves life. He who loves spontaneously wants the beloved to live. Crimes of love, when indeed there is love, are motivated by false, egocentric love. They no more merit our admiration or indulgence than any other crime.

[3] DYING FOR LOVE OF A "CAUSE"

Happily, death and love are conjoined at higher levels of human activity. Although men naturally desire to live and find death instinctively repugnant, they have in all ages and civilizations risked death for love of a cause, an ideal. Love, in fact, can sublimate death and abolish our fear of it.

In primitive human society, where individual consciousness was less developed, nothing was psychologically more normal than the sacrifice of life for what was thought to be the collective interest. Here, we cannot even speak of love in the strict sense of the word. The instinct for survival alone motivated such acts. Even in our highly individualized societies many men have consented to die for love of their country, which is a collective value. The poetry which Charles Péguy wrote in 1914, for example, inspired thousands of men and made death on the battlefield seem a beautiful thing.

It is well known that in 1939 French soldiers were far less disposed than in 1914 to go off to war, to sacrifice their lives for the defense of their threatened country. This can be explained in large part by the hypertrophy of individual consciousness in France during the decades preceding World War II. Because of this, many had become incapable of loving anything but themselves. However, there was another factor. The evolution of consciousness had transcended the national phase and attained a greater degree of universality. The love of pacifists and humanists embraced all of mankind, while the ideal of proletarian solidarity inspired millions of Communist workers. Quite normally, the idea of sacrificing their lives for love of country could not touch these men deeply. But the capacity of these same men for heroism and death in the name of a supra-individual good remained very real. This was proven by their resistance to the Nazi occupation. In that crisis, countless Frenchmen, from many different social and religious backgrounds, willingly engaged in a combat that was far more dangerous than the usual forms of warfare. Perhaps the professional soldiers and veterans of the war of 1914–1918 risked the perils of the Resistance for love of country, but the average combatant and particularly the young fought out of love of another ideal—or, as some would have it, another "myth."

It seems likely that the same is true of others who fought against the Nazi invader. The Polish and other Eastern European and Balkan countries which had recently won national independence were no doubt more motivated by patriotic solidarity than the countries of Western Europe. But even in these cases we may ask whether or not resistance to the German onslaught would have been so implacable if the latter had not constituted a grave threat to individual and collective freedom. This was clear with respect to Russia. At first many people welcomed the German troops as liberators from the tyranny of Stalin. That the supposed liberators were "foreigners" did not seem to raise any problems for the Ukrainians and other Soviet peoples. Only after they realized that the new oppression was worse than the old, did patriotism revive and the resistance come into being.

Another striking example of modern man's love of freedom was furnished by the Spanish Civil War. Thousands of men from countries all over the world volunteered their services and died in Spain because freedom was threatened there. To be sure, Anarchists, Communists, Democratic Socialists and Christians differed greatly in their understanding of freedom. Nonetheless, for several years the mythic strength of the word justified for all of them the sacrifice of their lives.

I am not arguing that love which defies death is in all cases perfectly pure. Occasionally there can be much hatred mixed with it. It is not at all impossible that the resistance included many men who were as much, if not more, motivated by hatred for the enemy than by love of freedom. Nor was their behavior toward the enemy always free of sadistic cruelty. But whenever I have had the opportunity to explore in some depth the motivation of those who fought in the Resistance it was clear that love and freedom were the predominant motives, even when they were not fully conscious. Hatred could explain their aggression against the enemy, but they exposed their own lives to the dangers of torture and death because their hearts vibrated with love of freedom.

Similarly, propaganda can persuade the majority of the

American people that their young men should die in Vietnam because they are convinced that freedom is threatened there by Communism.

It is important to stress that the majority of those who consent to die for their country, freedom, justice or any other transcendent ideal are by no means old men who are weary of life but young men whose love of life cannot be questioned.

[4]   MARTYRDOM

Psychologists see the most intimate and the most explicit relationship between death and love in martyrdom. In this case, pure love, exempt from all hatred and all unconscious release of aggressiveness, motivates men to accept and even desire death. Not only did the Christian martyrs, both at the time of the persecutions which victimized the early Church and during all subsequent persecutions, not hate their executioners, they prayed for them and ardently hoped for their conversion to the faith of Christ. They wanted their persecutors to share in the happiness of heaven which they believed in and desired with all their strength.

In the history of the origins of Christianity, martyrdom occupies a very important place. It contributed greatly to the reputation and diffusion of the new religion. Christians consented so readily to die for love of Christ, many of their contemporaries said, because they were in possession of certainties which others lack. The result was often a desire to know this religion and adhere to it.

Christianity has no monopoly on martyrs. Let us recall a sublime narrative from the Old Testament. When Palestine was ruled by Antiochus in the second century before Christ, many Jews, out of their love of the Law and Jehovah, heroically resisted the tide of Hellenization and died martyrs of their faith. "It came to pass also that seven brethren, together with their mother, were apprehended and required by the king to eat swine's flesh against the law, to which end they were tormented with whips and scourges. But one of them, who was the eldest, spoke thus: 'We are ready to die rather than transgress the laws of God, received from our fathers.' Then the king, being angry, commanded frying pans and brazen cauldrons to be made hot; which forthwith being heated, he commanded to be cut out the tongue of him that had spoken first and, the skin of his head being drawn off, to chop off also the extremities of his hands and feet, the rest of his brethren and his mother looking on. And when he was now maimed in all parts, he commanded him, being yet alive, to be brought to the fire and to be fried in the frying pan. And while he was suffering therein long torments the rest, together with the mother, exhorted one another to die manfully. . . Now the mother was to be admired above measure and worthy to be remembered by good men, who beheld her seven sons slain in the space of one day and bore it with a good courage for the hope she had in God. And she bravely exhorted every one of them in her own language. Being filled with wisdom, she joined a man's heart to a woman's thought . . ." (II Machabees 7). The mother was the last to be killed.

In this dramatic narrative the stress is as much on the mutual love of the brothers and their mother as on their common love for divine law. Moreover, these martyrs made no distinction between love of the law (which is to say of Jehovah) and their mutual love of one another. It was because the mother loved her children so deeply that she exhorted them to die for the love of Jehovah, being firmly convinced that the secret of their own greatest happiness was to be found in this love.

The Jewish faith is still capable of inspiring the kind of love that joyfully accepts martyrdom. This was proven over and over again during the Nazi persecution. Two novels with great documentary value are to be recommended in this context: *The Last of the Just* by the Jewish author André Schwartz-Bart and *Men Do Not Want to Die* by the Christian, Pierre Henri Simon.

Christianity, however, must be credited with establishing a transcendental relationship between death and love. It is in fact one of the most fundamental articles of the Christian faith that Christ, the Son of God, became man, suffered and died on the cross for love of God, his Father, and men, his brothers. He was not spared anxiety or agony, the poignant feeling of dereliction. According to his own words as reported by the Evangelists, he could have called upon "legions of angels" to avoid death. But he did not, for, as the Apostle John says, "no greater love hath any man than that he lay down his life for his friends." Of course, as every Christian knows, each of the Son of God's acts was of infinite value and would have been enough to redeem all the sins of the world. To many unbelievers and even believers, it seems cruel on God's part to have demanded His own son's death on the cross for the redemption of Adam's sin, which was after all very insignificant by comparison. But Christian tradition does not view the matter from this perspective. Golgotha was not merely a matter of justice and reparation but of overwhelming proof of love for mankind.

It can be said without fear of exaggeration that the whole of Christianity is founded on the mysterious bond that its founder established between death and love. Meditation on For the authentic Christian, death can never be separated from and imitation of this mystery are intrinsic to Christian sanctity.

love. "For to me, to live is Christ and to die is gain," writes
the Apostle Paul to the Philippians. To be sure, most fervent
believers experience instinctive "physical" fear of death, but
they hope to overcome it through love. It is from this perspective that we must read the testimonies of Polycarpus of
Smyrna, Ignatius of Antioch and other martyrs who gladly
embraced torture and death. They saw in this the best way of
showing their love for Christ and men. "Martyrs," wrote St.
Ireneus, "find comfort from their torments in the love of
Christ."

It is not surprising that the mysterious relationship Christian philosophy has established between death and love has
given rise to misunderstandings and abuses. Not without
reason, Christians have often been accused of not loving life
enough, of preferring the certainty of an afterlife which faith
promises them for the risks of this life. In the fourth century,
a mystical fraternity affirmed that it was not enough to consent to martyrdom when the enemies of Christ imposed it.
True Christians ought, in addition, to actively seek it out,
to provoke the authorities to kill them. If they could not
convince Roman officials to do this they beseeched passers-
by to martyr them. They succeeded in practically abolishing
the distinction between martyrdom and suicide. The Church,
through the voice of her authorized representatives, was quick
to condemn such perversions. "Polycarpus," wrote St. Cy-
prian, "gave the example of a martyr in the spirit of the
Gospel. Polycarpus waited to be delivered, exactly as did
the Lord. Each of us must be ready to confess the faith by
submitting to martyrdom, but no one ought to actively seek
it out."

I don't think there are many Christians today who would
deliberately invite martyrdom. Still, the confusion created

by the close connection between death and love has occasioned many serious errors over the centuries. The result has been an inadequately positive attitude toward life and the world, best summarized in the mystical image of the "valley of tears." Death was portrayed by preachers as a happy deliverance from the pains of life, as the supreme act of love. Little wonder that the faithful attached little importance to the things of the earth. Good Christians were urged to scorn life, to meditate daily on death and live as though they would die at any minute. Bossuet, in one of his celebrated funeral sermons, exclaimed: "O happy moment! Who does not desire death is no Christian!" This deviation is widely manifest in what little influence Christianity has on the institutions and morals of society.

Today, happily, we no longer share that mentality. The death of Christ on the cross for the love of men, of course, remains as always the central mystery of Christianity. But for most Christians today, meditation upon this mystery in no way implies a contempt for life in this world. Too, every Christian wants to make his death an act of love and it is customary for the dying person to offer his death for a noble cause. But death is now conceived as the fulfillment of life rather than its negation. The more we love life, the more we dedicate ourselves to its service. In this way we increase our chances of dying in a state of love, what the theologians call a state of grace.

A certain type of spirituality, which is called *Jansenist* but is in fact much older, considered it a weakness in the true believer to want to live a long time on this earth. It saw in such a desire a lack of love for Christ, a lack of esteem for heavenly beatitude. In pious conversation it was considered good taste to complain about the burdens of life and express the hope of joining Christ and his saints in heaven as soon as possible—although it is very probable that most of those who uttered such edifying propositions were not at all anxious to die. Today, thanks to our deeper awareness of the meaning of life in this world, the desire to live a long and happy life strikes even the most pious Christian not only as legitimate but as the normal expression of the life instinct. The Christian faith need not stifle or repress us. Today we understand better St. Paul's renunciation of his desire to join Christ in order to live for the glory of God. But there is this important difference: For Christians today, working for the glory of God no longer consists only in charitable works but in temporal activity as well.

Despite many similarities, there is a great psychological difference between martyrs and those who die out of love for a cause, an ideal. The martyrs in fact died not so much for an idea or a doctrine as for a very concrete Person whom they loved more than life itself. Unlike the partisans of a doctrine or a myth, they did not scorn life—either their own or those of others. In this perspective, the butchers of the Inquisition seem like "heretics" in the strict sense of the word; their love of God was perverted by dogmatic fanaticism. And fanaticism must never be confused with generosity. The martyr's love of Christ enables him to accept death joyfully, but the fanatical Inquisitors were intent upon the deaths of others.

The close relationship between death and love in the Christian conscience does not imply resignation to either life or death. It is to the point to insist upon this truth, for the too-famous virtue of "Christian resignation," at least as it is understood today, strikes the best minds of our time more as cowardice than as an admirable virtue. Love of life is in reality just as much in keeping with the Christian vocation as it is with our instinctual demands. It implies neither disinterest in nor detachment from the temporal, but an attachment and engagement that are both active and joyful. We should actively consent to death rather than merely resigning ourselves to it. Only in this way will we be able to transfigure what in the natural order is a biological necessity into a free, i.e., human, act.

[5]   I WOULD RATHER DIE . . .

If it is true that love can make death beautiful, it is equally incontestable that a life without love is intolerable. There are, of course, men who cling to life even though they don't love anyone and know that no one loves them. But most people would say with perfect sincerity, "I would rather die than live without love."

Depth psychology shows that most of those whose will to live is weak and who seek refuge in death from the difficulties and risks of life were unloved in their childhood or are, because of their neurotic conflicts, incapable of love.

Raymond, a thirty-year-old lawyer, dreams of death constantly. Funeral processions and cemeteries arouse strong emotions in him which he thinks ought to be attributed to his fear of death. But analysis indicates that he is, on the contrary, suffering from a kind of nostalgic *frisson*. In all of his dreams the cementery is associated with images of repose, well-being and tranquillity. He greatly regrets that his religion prohibits suicide. Yet he hopes that an automobile accident or some natural catastrophe will soon take him from a life he abhors to the point of boredom. It goes without saying that Raymond's preoccupation with death has paralyzed his capacity to act. He is doomed to failure in all of his enterprises because he undertakes them half-heartedly. "I suppose one must do something," he explains. Freudian psychoanalysis would speak of his death wish, of his unconscious desire to return to his mother's womb. But I interpret his case quite differently. In the first place, Raymond has never loved a woman; he has had some passing sexual experience but without emotional participation. Nor has he any friends. He never even had any when he was an adolescent. He wonders why no one loves him and then immediately explains that it is probably because they know he is incapable of loving. It soon came to my knowledge that Raymond had never been loved as a child or, what comes to the same thing, had never *felt* himself loved. His parents got on badly together. They were relatively advanced in years at the time of Raymond's birth, a birth that no one wanted. His six brothers and sisters were much older than he and took no interest in the "little brat" whose existence only complicated family life. He has no happy memories of childhood whatsoever. He had wanted to die while he was still very young, especially whenever he was punished or encountered some difficulty at school.

How could a psychologist fail to understand Raymond? Martyrs and the heroes of generous causes die out of love for what is dearer to them than their own lives; Raymond wants to die because his life is deprived of love and therefore of meaning. When, with the help of therapy, he becomes capable of loving and, by that fact, of being loved, his life instinct will be liberated from inhibitions. He will then not be tempted to flee life in death but will perhaps be able to die for love of someone or something.

[6]   LOVE—THE CONQUEROR OF DEATH

Death as a biological necessity, required by the laws of a universe in becoming, will always be a scandal to the human consciousness unless it can be metamorphosed into a free human act. In this, and not in some very hypothetical immortality in time, does veritable victory over death reside. Now, as we have seen, only love can effect such a metamorphosis. Moreover, the capacity and need for love in the human heart can only find total fulfillment when love has triumphed over death itself.

Gabriel Marcel has understood this in his penetrating analyses of existence. "Human love," he writes, " is nothing if it is not charged with infinite possibilities. If it is not to die it must remain open." He is speaking of an openness to a yet more powerful love than the love we call "human." A man who only loves his own life and the lives of those who are close to him is basically an unhappy man. However ingenious his attempts to make this life beautiful and passionate, he must nevertheless leave it one day, unable to sublimate his natural horror of death. I am not speaking here of "sublimation" in the Freudian sense. I use it in its current meaning of making sublime that which is naturally fearful. Only love is capable of doing this.

According to Berdyaev, our fear of death is due to the more-or-less confused feeling all men have when confronted with the abyss that separates time from eternity. Only love can bridge this abyss and thus conquer anxiety. But the Russian philosopher goes further. He states that death is necessarily unintelligible to rational thought. It is because modern Western man pretends to live "according to pure reason" that he feels so disarmed before death, which can only inspire him with horror. Only thinking that is permeated with love can see in death more than a biological phenomenon and discover its true meaning. We have already referred to the speculations of philosophers and theologians on death. Their efforts have contributed to our knowledge, but we must admit that they have done nothing to conquer the repulsion and horror that every man necessarily experiences when he ponders his inevitable destruction. Only love has proven powerful and clear-sighted enough to envisage, beyond the destruction of empirical existence, new possibilities of construction.

It may seem paradoxical to maintain that love of life and of all living things contributes most effectively to victory over death. At first sight, it would seem that the more one loves life the more he ought to detest what destroys it. Nonetheless, existential experience confirms our thesis. It is precisely the great lovers of life who encounter death with serenity and, in many cases, with joy. The death of St. Francis of Assisi was as joyous as his life. In fact, it was on his deathbed that he composed his *Hymn to the Sun,* one of the most beautiful tributes to life in world literature. And it is not only saints and mystics who evince such an attitude toward death; it can also be found among ordinary men and women.

When people really love one another, death cannot kill their love. It can only destroy what is by nature ephemeral; its dominion is limited to the corporeal. But authentic love always transcends the empirical order. Thus the beloved might die but the bonds of love are as strong as ever. I know an old woman whose son died of tuberculosis nearly forty years ago. With the passage of years her sorrow has, of course, diminished. She had other children whom she loved as much as her deceased son. But the latter is as alive in her heart today as he ever was. A well-known contemporary philosopher has publicly acknowledged the intensity of his love for his departed wife. He lives with her in a more perfect communion than when she shared his daily life. Because of this experience of love as a conqueror of death, the philosopher in question was for a time inclined to place great faith in mediums. He soon abandoned this position, however, and now accounts for his experience within a more authentic metaphysical and psychological framework.

In his well-known novel, *For Whom the Bell Tolls,* Hemingway describes a similar victory of love over death: "Thou wilt go now, rabbit," Jordan says to the dying Maria. "But I go with thee. As long as there is one of us there is both of us. . . . Whichever one there is, is both."

The persistence of love beyond death often makes remarriage difficult for widows and widowers. Not that we would recommend the ancient Indian custom which commands the widow to die on her husband's funeral pyre, but many feel that they are being unfaithful to their deceased partners when they remarry. Married priests of the Orthodox Church are not allowed to marry a second time. Psychologically, however, a new love is not irreconcilable with fidelity of affection toward a deceased partner. One of my friends is a happily remarried widower but makes no secret of his deep love for his deceased first wife. In fact, his present wife and her children share this sentiment.

There is nothing surprising in the fact that love can be purer and more authentic after the death of a loved one. In the terrestrial condition of man it is difficult if not impossible to preserve love from the dross of daily routine. The carnal condition almost inevitably tarnishes love's flame. Later we shall have occasion to discuss the important role our capacity to love beyond death plays in the belief in immortality. Let us note for the moment that many lovers and poets consider death a fulfillment of, rather than a threat to, love. It is capable of promoting the most intimate union of hearts. In countless mythologies, likewise, the magic love potion also brings death.

From a slightly different point of view, love's victory over death is magnificently portrayed in Dante's *Inferno*. In his imaginary visit to that place of damnation, the poet met many lovers who were damned because of the culpable nature of their love. Their lot was a sad one, to be sure, but infinitely preferable to other categories in hell. According to Dante, love persists even in hell and because of this lovers there have the great advantage of being able to suffer together. Unlike the pessimistic vision of a Sartre, the Christian Dante does not see hell as a totally hopeless place. For those who love one another there is still a possibility of communication.

Some "romantic" lovers find the ecstasy of love is so extraordinary, so unique, that they find it impossible to live in the shadows of daily life after having known it. They desire death with all their hearts in order to render this privileged moment eternal. St. Paul, Catherine of Siena, Theresa of Avila and many others found ordinary life painful after the ineffable experience of ecstasy. Other romantic poets express envy for those insects that die in the act of copulation.

One of the greatest Romantic poets, Novalis, has immortalized his love for his young fiancée, Sophia, who died before they were married. "Her presence was so palpable," he wrote, "that I believed she would appear any minute." He felt "unutterably happy" while communicating with his deceased love. Even if he had been able, he would not have brought her back to life. Rather, he wished to join her in death; and the poet seriously contemplated suicide. But gradually he grew accustomed to the mystical communion between himself and the deceased Sophia and no longer wanted to die. In fact, the day would come when he would be able to love another woman without feeling unfaithful to Sophia.

Nerval, speaking of a young woman he loved, wrote after her death, "She belongs to me much more in death than in life." Proust, likewise, loved Albertine more after she died because she could no longer oppose or resist him.

The death of the women they loved gave the romantic lovers freedom to idealize them as they pleased. Their imaginations no longer came up against the contingent reality of the other. According to reliable evidence, the Sophia that Novalis celebrates and who inspired some of his best poems bore little resemblance to the rather mediocre girl that the poet would have married.

I do not doubt the subjective sincerity of romantics when they exalt love in death. But my admiration for this kind of love is rather limited. There has to be something lacking in one's emotional make-up, indeed one's life instinct, for one to prefer the death of a loved one to her carnal and living presence. Such a lover perhaps lacks confidence in the creative and renovating power of love or doubts the depth of his passion. His love tends to be a cerebral and egocentric enjoyment; it is possessive and considers the loved one something that belongs to him. Like a petulant child, the romantic lover prefers to see his loved one dead rather than accept the risk that his love might fail. As for those who say that they do not want to live after the experience of amorous ecstasy, we may suppose (if they are sincere) that their exaltation inhibits their life instinct for some length of time. A love that is capable of triumphing over death and surviving the physical separation is one thing; a love that desires and provokes death is quite another.

V

The Meaning of Death

The taste for life gives instinct
a kind of general freedom. Like
the muscular instinct it is assured
by a certain quality of the élan vital,
neither too much nor too little.
Loss of it can lead to suicide.

—EMMANUEL MOUNIER

❦

[1] THE BEING-TOWARD-DEATH

ALL men realize that they are mortal as soon as they become self-conscious. Nor is there much hope that they will ever be anything other than mortal. Progress in hygiene and the medical sciences have appreciably diminished the infant mortality rate and prolonged the average life span. It is likely that further progress will be made in this domain, perhaps even doubling the present life expectancy. But we know full well that all we can hope to do is postpone the fateful moment. Whether I die at sixty or one hundred, my mortal condition remains unchanged.

Because death is certain and inevitable, many thinkers

127

feel obliged to question the meaning of life and see it as merely an absurd agitation. When Heidegger, for example, defines man as a *being-toward-death,* he is not content to affirm a mere biological fact but insists upon the absolute vanity of everything we do. When Camus says in *The Stranger,* "Destiny condemns us all to death," he shares a similar vision. In *The Myth of Sisyphus* he is even more explicit: "Because of death," he writes, "human existence has no meaning. All the crimes that men could commit are nothing in comparison with that fundamental crime which is death." To whom shall we attribute this fundamental crime? Nietzsche, who had deep roots in the Christian tradition, would probably accuse God the Creator. But Camus never had much connection with the Christian tradition. Thus for him there can be no personal responsibility for the "fundamental crime." He argues that death became a crime with the emergence of self-consciousness, which is to say with man. Thus it is a crime without a criminal. In this sense Camus, despite the many differences between him and a Heidegger or a Sartre, is an existentialist atheist. The human condition, far from being the summit of evolution, is fragile and unhappy because it inevitably implies consciousness of death.

The literary work of André Malraux shows that he, too, is fascinated by the idea of death. At every juncture of his life as an adventurer and revolutionary he has confronted it. *The Royal Way, Man's Fate, Man's Hope* and his other novels are in the final analysis so many narratives of the failure of man's initiatives and hopes. Human striving always ends in death. Malraux sees the world as a gigantic prison in which those condemned to death can find deliverance only in death itself. "Imagine a large number of men in chains," he wrote in *Man's Fate,* "and all condemned to death. Each day some of them are butchered before the others. Those who remain see their own destiny in the lot of their brothers. . . . This is the image of man's fate." Unlike the existentialists, Malraux does not think that man's consciousness of being mortal is an unhappy consciousness for metaphysical reasons. It is only within the perspective of the modern humanism of the West that awareness of his mortal condition makes man unhappy. In the name of man's dignity and freedom, Malraux observes, the West began by killing God, and then man discovered himself condemned to death. "In order to destroy God, and after having destroyed him," we read in *The Temptation of the West,* "the European spirit has annihilated everything which could oppose man. At the end of its efforts it found nothing but death." A Christian could readily agree with this psychological observation, with one difference, however. Malraux thinks the present state of affairs is irreversible and his vision of the human condition is consequently as despairing as those of Heidegger and Camus.

[2]   REVOLT OR DISTRACTION?

Emmanuel Mounier has said, "The ages of great vitality were indifferent to death." Ideally and globally, that is probably true. But we must admit that insofar as we can judge from literature and works of art, consciousness of death has been generally keen and poignant in all ages. The great artist Michelangelo (whom no one would suspect of having lacked vitality) confessed that all of his thoughts were overshadowed by death. Cicero wrote: "The life of a philosopher is a perpetual meditation on death. . . . To philosophize is to learn how to die."

Is it really inevitable and desirable for man to be always

conscious of his being-toward-death? I frankly confess for my part that I follow neither Michelangelo's example nor Cicero's advice. It is seldom that my thinking turns spontaneously to my mortal condition. External circumstances or events must constrain me to do so. Even then I think of it almost as though it were an intellectual problem that scarcely concerned me existentially.

According to Pascal, men, unable to cure death, hit upon the idea of not thinking about it in order to be happy. They "distract themselves", or as we pointed out in our first chapter, they relegate the idea of death to the unconscious. There it generally causes much harm and engenders an incomprehensible anxiety. Depth psychology confirms Pascal's intuition. The frenetic pursuit of pleasure—sensual as well as aesthetic and intellectual—is for many people an unconscious flight from their anxiety about death. I am thinking here of a well-known French woman intellectual whose three-volume autobiography seems to have been explicitly written to confirm Pascal's thesis. For decades this woman's life was a "distraction," a greedy pursuit of every kind of enjoyment—sensual, emotional and intellectual. Meditation upon death seems to have been the least of her concerns. But in the last volume of her memoirs she is as haunted by the thought of her old age and death as any of the heroes of Camus or Malraux. In fact she insists upon it much more than they do, and a veritable despair shows its face.

I am convinced that it is morbid to make meditation upon death an end in itself. When such meditation intensifies, as it did for many of the "romantics," our anxiety about death and serves as a pretext for avoidance of the struggles and joys of life, then we must do everything we can to avoid it, even if we must seek flight in "distractions." Meditation on death can only be recommended if it helps us transfigure death and give it positive meaning. It is no doubt in this sense that we must interpret Michelangelo's words quoted above.

Constant meditation on death is paralyzing for both action and life. On the other hand, nothing is accomplished by repressing the thought of death or trying to drown it in a sea of distractions. It is much better to confront the reality directly and openly admit that death is both an intellecual and emotional scandal. Only after we have done this will it be possible for us to sublimate it.

Death, as we have already said, is a necessity in a universe that is in a perpetual state of creative evolution. Let us try to imagine what the simultaneous presence of all the men ever born into this world would be like. Obviously our planet could not contain them all. Were it not for the fact of death, the evolutionary process would have been halted long ago. Death creates the indispensable conditions for subsequent generations to be born. Thus on the biological plane the destruction of the living is a *sine qua non* condition of the evolution of life. Only life itself is immortal in the biological order.

Still, these very rational considerations do not abolish the scandal of death. I must confess that I see no way of justifying or explaining the death of infants, deprived so early of the opportunity to take part in life's adventures, or the wholesale death brought about by famine, war, earthquakes or other natural or man-provoked catastrophes. We may distract ourselves from the problem raised by such events, but the problem remains in its entirety.

Must we then join the cohorts of the existentialists of the absurd? We have already had occasion to refer to Heidegger's work, which has been such a powerful influence on contemporary philosophy and literature. He sees death as the ultimate coronation of the nothingness that constitutes our being. The only intelligent thing to do is to confront courageously the sad reality of our nothingness.

Camus, Sartre, Malraux (not General de Gaulle's minister of culture but the revolutionary combatant of an earlier day who authored *Man's Fate* and *Man's Hope*) and many other spokesmen for the intelligentsia of the twentieth century share Heidegger's pessimism about life and death. They have appreciably intensified and dramatized the German philosopher's ideas, and since their books have enjoyed widespread popularity their influence has been much greater than that of the master. The French writers, however, are generally inclined to modify Heidegger's pessimism. They think that man, despite the odds, can do something other and better than stoically accepting his sad fate. They agree that life and death have no meaning in themselves but feel we can bestow meaning upon them. Not all men can do this, of course. But some, those who live *authentically,* can and they do so in the name of all by virtue of the mysterious human solidarity that these three French writers profess in common.

Camus, especially, refuses to passively submit to an absurd destiny and thus become its accomplice. He says No, and rebels against it. "Men do not deserve to suffer and die," he wrote. His ambition is to live without illusions and then die without regret, all in taking pains to "die well." But the human condition being what it is, death can be beautiful only in revolt. Just why this is the case Camus does not tell us. Perhaps he was thinking of the death he and his comrades risked each day in their clandestine resistance against the Nazi "plague." In his novel, *The Plague,* he wrote that each of us must sacrifice ourselves for all. But he adds immediately, "although I do not know why." His own death, in an ordinary automobile accident at the age of forty-seven and at a time when he had reached the summit of literary glory, seems to be an after-the-fact confirmation of the major themes of his philosophy of the absurd. In the end his death served no purpose; it was not even "beautiful" as it would have been had he died in combat against some "plague."

André Malraux is not a philosopher and there is no evidence that he ever read Heidegger. But the philosophy implicit in his novels is identical with that of Camus. Like Camus, Malraux entertains no illusions about life or death and refuses to be an accomplice of an absurd and cruel destiny. Again like Camus, he wants to die in a dignified manner, to cut a fine figure on that scaffold that is every deathbed. If he and the heroes of his best novels engage heroically in revolutionary combat, it is not because they have any illusions about the new world that will be constructed on the ruins of the old one they try to destroy. Death will be infallibly present in the new world as well. Rather, in revolutionary commitment Malraux' heroes protest against all possible orders in the world. This probably explains why Malraux joined the ranks of the militant anticommunists as soon as communism became the *established order* in many countries.

As for the real master of atheistic existentialism, Jean-Paul Sartre, his way of being lucid and refusing to be an accomplice of destiny consists in denying all seriousness to either life or death. He considers both of them cruel irony.

[3]   CHOOSING THE MEANING OF LIFE

Is man's mortal condition really as hopeless as the writers we have just quoted say it is? We know there is no hope of conquering the biological reality of death. Death and birth are correlative facts; both imply a mutation of an essential state. We could not abolish death without at the same time abolishing birth. We have only to imagine for a moment what the world would be like without either death or birth to realize that the present order of things remains the best possible. The only question that seems legitimate to ask is the following: Would it not be possible to experience death, our own death as well as those of others, as something other than a catastrophe and a definitive confirmation of the absurdity of existence?

We cannot consider death an autonomous event, independent of life. "Death," says Hegel, "cannot be reduced to a clinical or mechanical process. The exterior world does not 'cause' it; at most it provokes it. Death pertains to the irrecusable interiority of life." Even pessimistic thinkers make an effort to distinguish their conceptions of death from their ideas of life. It is precisely because they see death as the ultimate end of life that they attribute a character of irremediable absurdity to it. Others see life as an absurd vanity and conclude that death is the logical culmination of that absurdity. Thus everyone's idea of death is closely related to his general philosophy of the world and life.

It is, therefore, a question of knowing whether or not it is really necessary to see in death the *end* of life. We understand the word "end" in a double sense here: as the annihilation of life and also in Heidegger's sense of a being-toward-death, which is to say that life has no other end but death. Upon the answer to this question will depend our acceptance or refusal of the philosophy which proclaims the absurdity of life and death.

Everyone agrees that death can have meaning only on

condition that life does. And conversely, if life has a meaning, death must also. I often have occasion to interrogate people about the meaning of life—not, as a rule, on the meaning of life in general but on the meaning of their own lives. It is symptomatic that healthy and simple people often confess that they have never been questioned on this subject. For them it is quite evident that their lives, however modest they be, have a very deep meaning. They take this to be one of those basic truths that is never discussed, that can never be seriously doubted.

Bernard is a farmer, around fifty years old. He has little formal education but is endowed with a naturally keen and profound mind. He is curious about everything and reflects a good deal. It is always a pleasure for me to discuss the problems of human existence with him. One day I introduced him to the ideas of Sartre and Camus about the absurdity of life. He was quite surprised but in no way disturbed. "Are these men sane?" he asked me with some hesitation. "Don't people make fun of them for talking such nonsense?" Bernard works his land, sows and harvests, and cares for his livestock. He tries to raise his children the best way he knows how and lends assistance to his elderly parents. He also makes an effort to contribute to the common good. The sum of his occupations and responsibilities fills his life materially and gives it adequate meaning. To be sure, Bernard loves life and hopes to live as long as possible. But, he says, "we can die in peace when we have done our duty." It strikes me that this French peasant's attitude towards life and death is typical of simple, balanced people.

I am also familiar with the attitudes of those who are neither quite so simple nor quite so well balanced. My experience as a psychotherapist indicates that the most frequent cause of neurosis and other psychic difficulties is not to be found in unconscious sexual conflicts, as orthodox psychoanalysis affirms. This may have been the case in Freud's time in the puritanical society of Vienna and other cities. Today sexual taboos have lost much of their dominion, at least in the educated centers of the West, over man's sexual life and over his unconscious life in general. Perhaps one of the principal reasons why psychoanalytic treatment fails is because many analysts, in excessive fidelity to the doctrinal presuppositions of Freudianism, continue to look for the cause of neurotic conflicts where it as a rule cannot be found. I would argue that the most frequent cause of psychic disturbances today is the absence or loss of the meaning of life. In my opinion, the celebrated Viennese psychotherapist, Victor Frankl, was quite right to propose the discovery of the meaning of life as the principal task all effective psychotherapy should set itself. It is important, however, to insist on the fact that, contrary to what many believe, the meaning of life is not something that exists prior to its "discovery." As one of my young patients quite accurately remarked, it is up to each individual to give meaning to his own life. We must both know what this is and be able to achieve it.

Most of those who have recourse to the services of psychotherapists are unaware that the real cause of their difficulties and anxieties is a life that lacks meaning. They attribute their unhappiness to conjugal misunderstanding, professional failures or an unsatisfactory social life. Yet when their problems are looked into more carefully and without doctrinal prejudice it generally turns out to be the case that their meaningless lives are the real cause of their neuroses. Conjugal, professional and social difficulties are not causes but consequences of meaninglessness.

Mathilda, thirty-five years old, has been married for sixteen years and has three children. She complains bitterly about her state in life. She has nothing specific against her husband. Their sexual life is very normal and satisfying for both of them. And the family's material situation is excellent. Yet she says she cannot tolerate her husband and blames him for not making her happy. For several years she has been searching for a friendship to fill her emptiness. On several occasions she made advances to men she thought would be worthy of her admiration. In each case she thought she had found the perfect partner for the communication she so desperately needed. Because of her natural beauty and charm, each new friend soon became a lover. But this was not what she wanted. Discouraged by this approach to her problem she undertook all kinds of studies and dedicated much of her time to charitable organizations. This tack also failed to satisfy her. After having minutely analyzed what was wrong with her familial and other relations, she reached the despairing conclusion that her life had no meaning and was a merely empty agitation. She had married too young, before she was mature enough to ask questions about herself, others and life in general. As she matured intellectually and emotionally she grew more dissatisfied. She had in fact become quite neurotic. Only after therapy did she succeed in giving her life a meaning. Then her husband, children and sundry activities became fulfilling. Externally, her life was the same as it had been previously; but her own attitude toward it had been transformed.

The case of Marcel, a highly placed government official of forty, is somewhat similar. He had entered the civil service because his parents, with characteristic provincial thrift, wanted security for their only son. Marcel was very successful in his career because he worked at it to the exclusion of most other activities. When he had gone as far as his abilities permitted, he became painfully conscious of the emptiness in his life. He no longer took any interest in his work. He had never been socially ambitious and worked hard only to please his parents, who constantly reminded him of "all they had done for him." By the time Marcel had achieved success his parents were dead. Consequently, he no longer had any goal to pursue. He fell into an intolerable and agonizing state of boredom and sought to alleviate it in erotic entanglements. But these proved only momentarily satisfying and were followed by an even worse disgust for life. After an attempted suicide, he sought help in psychotherapy. Here again, the search for a meaning in life formed the basis of treatment.

Man can live for his children, for his country, for humanity, for art or science, or for the glory of God. What matters from a psychological point of view is that he live for something or, preferably, for someone. But, as we said earlier, this meaning, this justification for our lives, is not decreed from on high. It must continually be discovered anew. A false conception of man's vocation and the meaning of life is often the cause of feelings of failure and unhappiness. Many men and women complain of having missed their vocation and being as a consequence definitively condemned to mediocrity. In the final analysis, each man's vocation and the meaning of his life depends on his own free will.

Here we seem to be affirming a thesis dear to Sartre and other existentialists. These writers are quite right in stressing the liberty of choice that each of us must exercise in life. It is only through this freedom that we can confer meaning upon our lives and elevate them above mediocrity. But I part company with the existentialist conception of freedom on one important point: We should not arbitrarily give our lives one meaning rather than another. Life's meaning should be the outcome of our deepest convictions as well as the sincerest demands of our hearts. It is also important to take into account the concrete capacities and possibilities of each individual. Thus it is not enough to say to a disturbed person: "Become a monk or a communist; dedicate yourself to abstract painting or underdeveloped countries; what is essential is to have the illusion of doing something and feeling that one is useful." This kind of sceptical relativism cannot give true meaning to life. On the other hand, I am in perfect agreement with Dr. Jean Charon when he writes: "Each choice I make must be based on what I am and only on that."

[4] DEATH IN THE IMAGE OF LIFE

Instead of thinking of death as the end (in the double sense of that word) of life, I propose that we see it as the last act, the fulfillment of temporal existence. It would then follow that if we succeed in giving meaning to our lives, death would be by the same token meaningful.

Not that death will necessarily be an agreeable event for those whose lives are meaningful. They will by no means be exempt from anxiety about death. Christ, for example, knew the terrors of agony although this did not seem particularly shocking to the evangelists who reported it. Even though he is convinced that his life is in the service of a transcendent cause, a man may still regret that his mission must be interrupted. Nonetheless, it is not likely that such a man will consider his death a scandal, much less an absurdity. I have often noted that men who live intensely and know why they are alive are much more serene in old age and death. They accept the latter as the normal term of their maturation and achievements—and this quite independently of their belief in personal survival. Conscious of having lived for something and having been fulfilled in life, they are capable of spontaneously conferring meaning on that ultimate act of their lives which is death.

The meaning of death is still more obvious when man is aware of dying *for* something or someone. We have already mentioned the important psychological difference between French soldiers in the first and second World Wars. The first risked their lives for reasons of patriotism, which they considered an authentic value. They were proud of taking part in the battles of the Marne and Verdun; their families were likewise proud of them. In 1939, particularly in light of the German-Soviet pact, large numbers of Frenchmen considered the war none of their business. They saw it exclusively as an affair between governments and capitalist interests. When Maurice Thorez, the French Communist leader, deserted, few were shocked and he continued his political career after the war as though nothing had happened. This is because in the time between the two wars patriotism had ceased to be a universally recognized value. The lamentable French debacle in 1940 can be explained less by the technical superiority of the adversary than the French refusal "to die for nothing". Nazi propaganda, on the other hand, convinced millions of young Germans that they were going to die for the allegedly sacred cause of the German race and blood. Some years later many of these same Frenchmen fought against the Nazi occupation forces in extremely perilous conditions. They had come to see the cause of *freedom* as one worth dying for. The walls of prisons and concentration camps have yielded a moving anthology of graffiti proclaiming the faith and resolution of those who died for this cause. I have known a number of men who had been condemned to die but escaped at the last moment. One young man, a Marxist and atheist, had awaited execution for two months. He felt in no way rebellious or anxious; on the contrary, he was proud to have been chosen by a mysterious destiny to die for freedom at the age of twenty-eight. He could offer no convincing rational explanation for his firm conviction that his death, far from being absurd and useless, would effectively serve a cause he believed in. His conviction was rooted in deeper parts of his being than reason. Another young Communist intellectual who had been condemned to death wrote in his journal: "I could only with difficulty imagine that I would soon die. From a rational point of view, my death meant nothing more than the definitive termination of a life that had been brief but very intense. But it was difficult, indeed impossible, for me to admit that it would serve no purpose, that everything would be reduced to nothingness. A none-too-orthodoxly Marxist voice whispered that my death itself would serve the cause for which I had lived, that my blood would in some way be fecund. The Marxist dialectic cannot explain this efficacy. But when one is awaiting execution doesn't he have the right to a few small dialectical heresies?"

A believer would not behave much differently under similar circumstances. Contrary to what those who think of religion as a kind of business transaction between man and God might suppose, the legion of Christians who sacrificed their lives under a Nero, a Stalin or a Hitler were not motivated primarily by the thought of rewards in the hereafter. They did not question the reality of eternal life and no doubt expected to share in it. But from a psychological point of view their behavior while awaiting death differed little from that of their atheist comrades. Both were prepared to die for a cause which they believed to be well worth the sacrifice of their lives. Both were, moreover, convinced that their death was more than an absurd end of their struggles—that it was, in sum, a mysterious consecration. In the Nazi death camps, where chances for escape were slim, many Christians and atheists learned to mutually esteem one another. They learned that the "other" took his faith or his ideal seriously and was willing to die for it. The awareness of dying for something great and noble strips death of its absurd character, not only for those who die but for those who survive as well. I recall a young pregnant wife whose husband had been shot by the Germans in the spring of 1944. I met her on the very day she had learned of her husband's death. She wept, of course, but there was no despair in her sadness. In the midst of her tears she proudly told her three-year-old son how his father had died for freedom. Her sorrow was essentially different from that of another young woman of my acquaintance whose husband was accidentally killed in an air raid. She protested that she could never understand why he had to be in that precise place at that precise moment. She saw her husband's death and the inconvenience it implied for her and her children as scandalously unjust. She blamed the Germans who occupied the country, the English who had been responsible for the air raid and God who permitted such evils to happen. The wife of the man who died for his convictions, on the other hand, was not even bitter toward her husband's executioners.

There can be a difference between the subjective meaning of death and its objective value. The young Nazis, spellbound by the propaganda of Rosenberg and Goebbels, often greeted death with as much exaltation and disinterested courage as the best of those who died for liberty, even the Christian martyrs. From a psychological point of view, they also gave their lives a meaning and were convinced that by dying for their "Führer" they were doing something noble. But morally there is good reason to question the value of such deaths. From an individualistic point of view, we might be tempted to ignore the objective worth of the cause for which they died and stress the subjective intention. The philosophy of the "gratuitous act" which was popular with the young between the wars encouraged this attitude. But to isolate the individual and the meaning of his life in this manner is contrary to man's true nature. Personal destiny cannot be separated from the destiny of the human community. We can, to be sure, grant the courage of the young Nazi or that of a criminal in the electric chair. But neither has a right to our admiration.

It is the duty of each one of us, particularly the duty of educators, to bring about the integration of the subjective, individual meaning of life with the communitarian significance of human existence.

[5]   THE DEATH OF THE "ORDINARY" MAN

When a psychologist describes the human soul, his examples are usually chosen from among neurotics. This is partly because his profession brings him into contact with many neurotics; it is also partly because neurotics exhibit strong reactions which in the "normal" man are only found in an attenuated form. This applies to the topic under consideration here. To make clear the meaning of life and its fulfillment in death I have chosen most of my examples from among the martyrs of faith, and those who fight for their country, freedom and justice. This procedure can be justified dialectically because in such instances the meaning of death is particularly evident. But we must beware of hasty generalizations. On several occasions I have denounced the serious methodological error which many Freudians commit. Because they encounter incestuous tendencies and other "perversions" in their patients they systematically conclude that these same proclivities are inherent in every sick psyche and, furthermore, constitute the very essence of our psychic life. Similarly, with respect to our present subject, it would be a grave error to give the impression that only a violent or heroic death can be meaningful. If this were the case very few men would be able to escape the scandal and absurdity of death. Thus it is important to insist on the fact that heroes and saints are not the only ones whose lives and deaths have meaning. The life of the so-called "ordinary" man has great meaning too, although it is often more difficult to discern.

I spoke earlier of the simple peasant, Bernard, who never doubted that his life had meaning or that death was the normal fulfillment of life. One day while he was showing me his parents' grave in the village cemetery, he spoke quite naturally of his own burial place for which space had already been reserved beside his parents.

Leonardo da Vinci spoke wisely when he said: "Just as a well-filled day gives joy to sleep so too does a well-spent life give joy to death." To be sure, every healthy man loves life and hopes it will be as long and joyous as possible. This seems to be what da Vinci means by a "well-spent life." For the man who uses his life well, death seems spontaneously, without the least pretense, to come not as the destruction, but as the fulfillment of life. Simple people rarely think of death as a violence, imposed from without by some force inimical to life. They see it as the normal fulfillment of life and it is altogether natural for them to call it the "last sleep."

I obviously do not contest the great difficulty, indeed sometimes the impossibility, of discovering the deep meaning of each individual's death. For that matter, the meaning a man gives to his life is not always easy to see. What meaning, for example, could be given to the accidental death of a young man of twenty? How can we honestly see his death as the fulfillment of life when he had scarcely begun to live? What are we to think of the death of children? And those unfortunates who never truly lived? Since the meaning of life, and therefore of death, depends on man's free choice, it follows that he who is not capable of such a choice cannot give meaning to either his life or his death. Thus we are forced to conclude that only those who are capable of freedom can give meaning to their life and death. As for others, we must admit that we cannot, at least in the present state of our knowledge, understand the meaning of their life or death. Perhaps we are to see them as inevitable lapses in the process of creative evolution spoken of by Bergson and Teilhard de Chardin.

[6]   DEATH AS THE FULFILLMENT OF THE PERSON

We need not be afraid of death, but it is difficult not to think about it. Whether we admit it or not, it would seem (so far as I am able to judge by the confidences I have received) that after a certain age, generally around sixty, it is impossible not to think about death at least at certain times. The death of friends is a common occurrence at that age. When an older man makes plans for the future he knows that little time remains to carry them out. In rural areas, where the consciousness of familial continuity is greater, this kind of inhibition probably plays a lesser role. An old farmer continues to plant trees and care for his crops in the knowledge that his son or grandson will profit by his efforts. But in cities we are more conscious of our individuality and take little consolation in the knowledge that our descendants will benefit by what death prevents us from enjoying ourselves. This state of mind explains why governments, even in communist countries, find it increasingly difficult to persuade citizens to make sacrifices for future generations. This is why there is a decrease in long-range savings and investments and a constant increase of expenditures on goods for immediate consumption.

If it is true, as Emmanuel Mounier writes, that "ages of high vitality are indifferent to death," we must admit that our age is scarcely a vital one. Modern man does not meditate on death in the manner recommended by Plato. He is solely concerned with postponing the fateful moment as long as possible and at any price. Books offering recipes for longevity abound. Countless men and women deprive themselves of the most natural pleasures of life in the more-or-less fallacious hope of postponing the hour of death. Medical attempts to artificially prolong the lives of the dying by a few days or even a few hours meet with general approval, even when a cure is known to be impossible.

But it would be a mistake to see in this contemporary will to live as long as possible proof of a passionate love of life. In fact experience shows that the less a man *lives,* in the proper sense of that word, the more he clings to life. It is not psychologically true that those who have lost interest in life find death easier to accept. It is the verdict of experience that the more intensely a man lives the easier it is for him to die. Emphasis on the miseries and deceptions of life in no way makes death easier to accept.

The ancient Greeks thought that to die young, in the full flush of our powers, was an exceptionally good piece of luck, a blessing from the gods. Latter-day Romantics like Byron and Charles Péguy proclaim the same thing. They, too, believed that a long life without glory was not to be envied. Only the greedy and those without the courage to take chances would prefer such a life to a heroic death. I am personally inclined to think that it is better to live intensely for thirty or forty years than to vegetate for a hundred. But a long life that is well lived is desirable. We express admiration for a Mozart, who wrote such magnificent music in a brief lifetime, but Beethoven wrote many of his finest works in old age. Blaise Pascal, Soren Kierkegaard, Franz Kafka and Emmanuel Mounier died young but their accomplishments were considerable. On the other hand, Goethe, Bergson, Blondel and Jung wrote some of their most important books in the last periods of long lifetimes. These examples show that it is altogether pointless to say when a man's creative output is ended. The important thing is to live well. It is a sure mark of decadence in a civilization when a large percentage of men are willing to sell their souls, their bodies and their honor for a few more years of life, especially when they have no idea how life should be lived.

From time immemorial, men have admired those who faced death fearlessly. The heroes of history and all mythology are as distinguished by the way they died as by the nobility of their lives. Quite rightly, we consider courage in the face of death the sign *par excellence* of the soul's strength. It is irrefutable proof that there are values which are more important than life itself, that the finest flower of life is its transcendent dimension. But only those who are deeply aware of total humanity can appreciate life's transcendence. Without this awareness, we would normally consider our individual lives the most precious of values. Those who argue that the fear of death is the direct and inevitable consequence of man's consciousness of his individuality are not altogether right. Fear of death existed in primitive societies and seems to be at the origin of the diverse magical rites intended to exorcise this fear. And, as we have noted earlier, even animals are not exempt from a certain "physical" fear of death. Resistance to death is one of the normal reactions of the life instinct. What distinguishes the excessive individualism of modern Western society is the paralyzing fear of death that prevents many from living deeply. We are so conscious of being an *individual* that we have totally lost the consciousness of our appurtenance to the *whole*.

It is far from my intention to recommend the dissolution of individual consciousness into some nebulous Whole in the manner of certain pantheist or neo-pantheist religions and philosophies of the Orient. Even supposing that this was the primitive condition of men, a return to it would be utopian, not only impossible to realize but in no way desirable. The process of evolution is irreversible. We must seek the solution to our problems in the future rather than in the past.

Narrow individualism must be transcended by *personalism*. I mean by this the synthesis of what is "true" in both the primitive collective consciousness and its dialectical negation by individualism. The individual denies the Whole or at least resists it; but a person knows that he is and wants to be a part of the Whole. He is not afraid of losing something of himself when he sacrifices himself for a cause that is greater than he. Death is the destruction of the individual; but it is the supreme fulfillment of the person. The history of the individual is definitively closed when he takes his last breath; nothing can be added or subtracted from what he is at that moment. On the other hand, the true personality of a man is frequently not revealed until long after his death. The individual Socrates died in the year 399 B.C. shortly after taking the hemlock. But who would deny that Socrates' personality is as alive for students of philosophy today as it was for those of ancient Athens?

Teilhard de Chardin put the question we are discussing here in these words: "In the light of the convergent fires of co-reflection is the wall of death always as high and as insurmountable as it first seems to the isolated view of our reason?" The answer to this question is obvious to me. I would only substitute the word "co-consciousness" for "co-reflection," to include both knowledge and love. For it goes without saying that if we are to give a meaning to our life and death, we must enlist the services not only of our minds but of our hearts, our capacity for love.

We pointed out earlier that what made the deaths of the early Christian martyrs such joyful events, so much so that even torture failed to frighten them, was not, as is often believed, the hope of individual reward. It was the firm conviction of belonging to a community of brothers and the belief that their martyrdom would be singular proof of their love for that community. The blood of the martyrs was in fact looked upon by the Church as the seed of holiness. Those who die for reasons of patriotism, freedom and justice are perhaps less conscious of the ties that bind them to the community, but this sentiment must be operative at least unconsciously or they would not be able to renounce their lives.

Whether or not they believed in personal survival, none of them could believe that he was destroying himself in dying for a transcendent cause. Again, we agree with Teilhard de Chardin: "In the spiritualist [i.e., personalist] vision of evolution . . . death, for the moment, and despite the redoubtable transformations it brings about, is really exorcised—its venom has been removed from the heart of things." It is likewise in this personalist and communitarian perspective that we must understand Socrates' refusal to save his life at the price of disobedience to the laws of Athens, as well as Christ's refusal to deny his "hour." In an individualistic perspective, their behavior, and that of all martyrs and others who give up their lives voluntarily, is seen as the equivalent of suicide. Thus writers at the end of the nineteenth and the beginning of the twentieth centuries, a period when individualism was rampant, greatly misunderstood the deaths of Socrates and Christ. Nietzsche, who was so often at odds with and ahead of his time, was scandalized by the crucifixion of Christ.

Man questions himself on the meaning of his life precisely because he knows that he is mortal. If we believed that we were immortal we would no longer question the meaning of our lives. We saw in the first chapter that this was the case with Count Fosca. Life and death are so intimately related that it is impossible to establish the sense of one without being confronted with the meaning of the other. Plato, who defined life as an apprenticeship for death, emphatically recommended meditation on death in order to discover the meaning of life. I personally would be more inclined to adopt Spinoza's point of view. He advised meditation on life in order to grasp the meaning of death. However, properly understood, both forms of meditation have the same result. Modern man, it is true, is more familiar with Freud and Heidegger than with

Plato. Thus he has subjective reasons for fearing that meditation on death will only lead to a depreciation of life. In any case, there is little doubt that if our experience of life is intense and dramatic, if we are convinced that we do not have the right to waste the little time allotted to us, it is because we know that we are mortal. If we did not know that we would die one day, life would be little more than a boring routine.

Thus our position is at the opposite pole from the pessimism of those existentialists who teach that nothing in life has any meaning because man knows he is mortal. "To get drunk alone or lead nations comes to the same thing," says Sartre. All human activity is mere sound and fury. It seems to me that we could only think this way if we ignored our mortal condition. Why do today what could be just as well done in a thousand years. This is the philosophy of *mañana* which is said to be dear to the Spaniards. On the other hand, because we know we are mortal, we necessarily learn our limits in time and space. We must do everything we can to transcend these limits, and this can only be done by living well. Consciousness of death seems, in fact, to be one of the essential factors in human progress. As Louis Lavelle perceptively observes: "By threatening our future, death teaches us to give a plenary and absolute value to the present." It renders avarice useless and enables us to control our ambitions. A Greek proverb says, "Hold no man happy until he is dead." Death poses the question of the meaning of life in all of its breadth and depth, for the end of an activity always reveals its meaning. Let us say, then, with Goethe, that man must himself *accomplish* his own act of dying, thus refusing to accept it as an inevitable defeat.

VI

Death, Where Is Thy Victory?

Death, like birth, is only
a transformation.
—LEIBNIZ

To give meaning to our death, to make of it an act of freedom through love, is certainly to accomplish a great deal. It enables us to experience life as the realization of a task rather than a vain and absurd agitation. But it is still not enough. For one thing, not everyone is capable of giving meaning to his life and death. Human existence, taken in a collective as well as an individual sense, cannot be truly justified unless life has the last word. And death, no matter how rich in meaning and significance, cannot satisfy this condition. It is important, therefore, to inquire into the possibility of this kind of victory over death.

I am not, of course, talking here about some elixir of longevity. No matter how long we live, we must sooner or later die. Even if we were to discover a way of assuring immortality in time, the problem would not be solved. I have already referred to the practically insoluble problems that would be posed by the indefinite prolongation of human life. Medical science is now in a position to stamp out the last of those plagues which are responsible for a high percentage of deaths in Asia, Africa and South America. Although naturally happy about this new step forward in science, most sociologists are anxiously wondering what advantage millions of men would find in being condemned to die of hunger rather than an epidemic. What would it be like if death were altogether abolished? We must resign ourselves to the fact that our iife can be no more than a function of the universal becoming.

If there is any hope of conquering death, it must be realized otherwise than by the indefinite prolongation of life in space and time. We can only give substance to this hope by trying to answer the question, "What is man?"

[I]   THE HUMAN REALITY

"After death everything comes to an end, even death," Seneca taught, with the intention of providing a means of overcoming the natural fear of life's end which generally affects even the unhappiest of men. And Kant wrote: "Where there is no time there can be no end either," meaning that since time in his philosophy is only one of the *a priori* categories of the mind, death can do no more than destroy our conception of time. I do not propose to discuss the worth of these theories here. I am only interested in determining the extent to which such speculations enabled these philosophers and those who followed them to conquer the fatality of death. And I must admit I have never met anyone who found them convincing.

The real question here is whether the human reality is or

is not essentially different from its biological reality. The position of materialism, which long reigned as the uncontested master of Western science and even today has many adherents, is well known. Materialism recognizes that man is different from other living species by reason of his self-consciousness, his freedom, his speech and other psychological faculties. But this can be accounted for by the fact that his brain is more highly developed. No one any longer holds that "the brain secretes thought in the same way that the liver secretes bile"; still, this is what the materialist doctrine basically contends. Then, since the brain disintegrates after death, man has no chance of conquering death. He must resign himself to disappearing as a person (which materialists do not distinguish from the individual) and content himself with serving the species to which he belongs and in which he will survive, at least for a time.

A serious man of science, Teilhard de Chardin examined the materialist position with his customary intellectual honesty. He entered fully into that point of view and asked himself whether or not man could accept the finality of death and console himself with the thought that his effort would contribute to a larger humanity, better balanced and more consistent than himself. I have often asked this same question of those who do not believe in a life after death. Many answer that they are quite happy in the knowledge that they have in some small way contributed to the growth of total man, of mankind. For this ideal, men of science renounce many pleasures in life and expose themselves to a thousand dangers. The Marxist goes still further. He not only sacrifices himself for a happy future which he can never share in, he also thinks it quite normal and legitimate to impose similar sacrifices on others, on whole nations, even against their will.

I shall now set forth some reasons why I cannot accept the materialist hypothesis. I do not doubt that we belong to "a larger humanity, better balanced and more consistent" than ourselves. It is consoling and encouraging to know that our labors in this life, often executed at the price of great privation and suffering, will not have been in vain, that generations to come will profit by them. We do not accept the saying, "After me the deluge," which well sums up the philosophy of a certain kind of individualism.

But awareness of being a more or less important part of the human, and even cosmic, Whole does not resolve the problem under discussion. Even a philosopher like Maurice Merleau-Ponty, who was far removed from any religious faith, recognized that "there is a center of consciousness in virtue of which we are not of this world." Moreover, this is not merely a question of resignation to individual death. Mankind itself will eventually perish—as a result of either a man-caused catastrophe or a cosmic cataclysm such as the cooling of the earth. If there is no hope of survival for the individual, then there can be no hope of survival for mankind as a whole. Human achievement would be doomed to failure with the extinction of the race. If we clearly comprehended this eventuality we would be discouraged from doing anything. If we adopted this perspective we should have to agree with those who say that it is a crime to bring children into the world because in so doing we are contributing to the nefarious work of death.

[2] A BASIC INTUITION

Human consciousness has always refused to admit the final and definitive failure of man himself and, consequently, affirmed the universal process of evolution and growth. "Physical" fear of death is greatly diminished by the universal conviction that all will not end with death. As we noted earlier, it was, historically, the negation of immortality that gave rise to the fear of death. Here we are talking about something quite different, namely, man's *intuition* that he is more than a biological entity; that he is in addition a *soul* and a *spirit*. Conceptions of this soul or spirit obviously differ with different peoples and civilizations, but they are all rationalizations of that act of basic faith which is founded on intuition. The latter is a synthetic function of the human psyche, more or less comparable to instinct in animals. It is not the negation of reason, nor does it contradict reason; rather it operates in a domain inaccessible to reason. It grasps reality in its totality. It is a normal function of the psyche and is always operative unless impeded by obstacles. And one of the principal obstacles to the normal functioning of intuition is the excessive intellectualization of modern Western culture. This is why so many of our contemporaries have lost the sense of true reality and live alienated lives.

Plato's philosophy is probably the best synthesis of the ancient belief, shared by most peoples, in the primacy of the soul. The bonds which unite the soul to the body are merely accidental and due to a metaphysical, if not a historical, fall. In a well known image the soul is in the body much as "a pilot is in a ship," which is to say the two are only extrinsically related. Thus the weaknesses and miseries of the body, indeed its complete disintegration after death, do not seriously affect the soul.

Contemporary insights into the human reality make it impossible to follow Plato in all respects, the grandeur of his vision notwithstanding. The relationship between the self and the body is far more substantial than Plato would have granted. Today we are aware not only that we *have* a body but that we *are* our bodies. Many are so convinced of this that they cannot imagine themselves to be anything more than a body. This is undoubtedly an excessive reaction against the exaggerated claims of a certain kind of disincarnated spirituality. Even Christian spirituality, influenced far more by neoplatonism than it has ever admitted, long held in contempt the body and terrestrial values. Preachers and pious writings went even further than the theologians, pushing the latters' abuse of logic to its extreme consequences. According to them, only cowardice or weakness keeps man from trying to extricate himself from all carnal and temporal attachments, which distort his true reality, namely, the soul. The Hellenized Jew, Philo, writing at about the time of Christ, said, "There is a twofold death: one concerns man in general, the other the soul in particular. The former consists in the separation of body and soul. The death of the soul, on the other hand, is the destruction of virtue and the appropriation of wickedness." I am not prepared to discuss the extent of Philo's influence on the early Christian thinkers, but it is clear that they too were intellectually formed by the masters of neoplatonism. Thus it is not surprising that so many Christians have professed, and still profess, a conception of the relationship between body and soul that is very like Philo's teaching. It was by sin, that famous "original" sin, that death entered the world, say the Christian writers and preachers. Despite a certain confusion in their terminology, they cannot be talking about the death of the body. Even saints die, and the abolition of the reign of sin by Christ's death on the Cross did not end corporeal death. The Virgin herself, although miraculously preserved from original sin, was not spared the death of the body. It must therefore be spiritual death, much as Philo conceived it, with which Christian doctrine is concerned. The confusion between the two stems from the awkward fusion of Jewish biblical realism and Plato's idealism. Judaism expressed no interest in the state of the soul separated from the body and could scarcely conceive of such a state.

I assert unequivocally that man *is* truly his body. Since, on this view, we must be vitally interested in its fate there can be no place for contempt or even detachment. But a basic intuition, anterior to all rational constructs, teaches us that we are something other, and more, than our bodies. Nothing authorizes us to doubt the validity of this first intuition. As Jean Charon, one of the most outstanding scientific thinkers of our time, has shown, all of our irreducible certitudes are founded on these basic intuitions. Because of the evidence of such intuitions, the normal man has no doubt about his own existence or the existence of the world about him of which he recognizes himself to be a part. The contortions of idealistic philosophy gave rise to the conditions in which such evidence could be doubted. It pains me to think that Descartes had to resort to his celebrated *Cogito* to convince himself of his own existence.

Man's consciousness of being more-than-a-body is the locus of thought and love, of all that constitutes the specificity of the human person. We call it *soul* or *spirit*. Not many physiologists today would hold that the spirit is "nothing more" than a function of the brain. Most scientists would agree with Jung, who said: "The psyche, as it is manifested in and through our experience, is bound to our physical nature, but this does not imply a biological dependence." The nineteenth-century scientist who failed to find any soul with his scalpel would seem a slightly more than ridiculous figure today. The soul is not limited by space and time, the "categories" of bodily movement.

There is of course a scientific psychology, based on physiology, which studies and measures different psychic activities. But it cannot tell us anything about what might exist beyond the physical basis of these activities. Only a psychology that incorporates the evidence of intuition can render this service. This precious faculty should never be stifled. As we noted, it is the excess of rationalization which endangers intuition. Let us insist once again on what we take to be an evident truth: namely, intuition is not opposed to reason but constitutes with it a harmonious synthesis of our modes of knowing. Pure intuitionism would be as incapable of attaining total reality—even the total reality of the soul—as pure rationalism.

[3] THE IMMORTALITY OF THE SOUL

It would seem that death is as radically final for man as it is for animals. Both are subject to disintegration and corruption. To prove the immortality of the soul—in which most men believe in one form or another—philosophers and theologians have elaborated different theories. For centuries the West relied principally on the so-called "rational" proofs of Aristotle, Aquinas, Anselm, Descartes and Kant. They proved the immortality of the soul on the basis of its substantiality, unity and spirituality. I have no desire to discredit these "proofs"; they seemed to have been intellectually satisfying for large numbers of people over a long period of time. But, rightly or wrongly, we are much less convinced today of the infallibility of logical reasoning than were men of former ages who thought it capable of reaching transcendental truth.

Among the many educated people with whom I have discussed this subject, I have not met one who feels peremptory force in these arguments. Those who believe in immortality do so on other grounds. Those who do not, find the proofs unconvincing. Speaking personally, I studied the proofs for the immortality of the soul when I was a philosophy student. I could not refute them, but they did not convince me either. Ten years later, when I came to *believe* in the immortality of the soul, I accorded these proofs an *a posteriori* value.

Modern man is not susceptible to conviction by logical or scientific reasoning alone. Bergson's philosophical work was a generous attempt to demonstrate, by the methods of modern science, the irreducibility of the human spirit to bodily organs. He taught that man's soul is the principle of intelligence, memory, freedom and love. In the exercise of these faculties the soul enjoys an undeniable independence from the body; it is, therefore, legitimate to suppose that it will not perish with the body. Like many men of my generation, I was greatly influenced by Bergson's philosophy. It contributed enormously to my later belief in the soul and its immortality. Bergson had a similar influence on a number of other young intellectuals, notably Charles Péguy, Jacques and Raïssa Maritain. On the other hand, scientists have contested the properly scientific value of Bergson's arguments and, of course, they have every right to do this.

Today, I am inclined to think that it is impossible to prove the immortality of the soul scientifically. Science operates within the framework of space and time, which is obviously not the realm of the spirit. Rational or scientific "proofs" must be regarded as efforts to translate a thinker's spiritual intuition into the language and mentality of a given age. The immortality of the soul is, in Bergsonian terminology, "an

immediate postulate of consciousness." Which is to say, all
ideas issuing from immediate experience are necessarily un-
demonstrable.

Since philosophy and science shed little light on the subject
under discussion, might we hope to find more help in the
direct experiences of the many people who believe their souls
are immortal? There is, for example, communication with
the dead through mediums. There is the fear of ghosts, modern as well as primitive. The folklore of all countries contains
innumerable stories of haunted houses. This evidence, to be
sure, must be examined in a highly critical spirit, but to
dismiss it purely and simply strikes me as a peculiar exercise
of the scientific mind. Men of the stature of William James,
Henri Bergson, Aldous Huxley and Gabriel Marcel did not
consider it beneath their dignity to seriously examine such
evidence. The British Society for Psychical Research, which
specializes in the study of what it calls "parapsychological"
phenomena, includes many well known scientists.

Many so-called "spiritualist revelations" can be explained
by the dislocation of personality, a disturbance that is well
known to modern psychiatry and depth psychology. Such
"revelations" are projected memories or unconscious fabrica-
tions, whether on the part of the medium himself or one of
the participants in the seance with whom the medium has
succeeded in establishing a kind of subconscious dialogue.
Thus Victor Hugo was convinced that he spoke with Shake-
speare, Dante, Pascal and other long-deceased celebrities. He
even believed that he wrote under their inspiration. But, by
some happy chance, all of these geniuses expressed ideas that
were in every case those of the author of *Notre Dame de Paris*.
To draw any conclusions from this example would be dangerous. Moreover, other mediums have drawn confirmation for

their ideas (quite different from those of Victor Hugo) from the same sources. It is more reasonable to presume that the inspiration came from Hugo's unconscious energies rather than from a realm beyond the tomb.

Still, I would not want to conclude that *all* communications with departed spirits are projections of this kind. Some of the evidence I have examined is very disturbing, even for one reluctant to give credence to this sort of thing. When a sick mother claims to have spoken with her prematurely deceased son, I readily discern the mechanisms of projection at work. But when this same mother says her son urgently recommended to her prayers a certain young man whom she has never heard of but a few days later learns that he is to be tried and perhaps condemned to death by a military court, I admit that this is disturbing to say the least. And I could adduce a number of other well documented facts which are equally disturbing.

Yet I would be hesitant to see in even the least suspect accounts of communication with the dead an argument in favor of the soul's immortality. Furthermore, the majority of the stories concerning mediums that I have heard are quite beside the point. As we shall point out in the next chapter, they do not tell us anything about the lives of these separated souls, nor can we be convinced of the supernatural origins of such communications. Even the most probable instances are perhaps no more than psychic phenomena which our present techniques cannot account for. In any case, what spiritualist communications and parapsychology really seem to establish is the fact of telepathy, which shows that the spirit can act independently of the body and the laws which regulate its activity. While such experiences cannot count as proofs for the immortality of the soul, I think they at least confirm this as a probability. Thus we agree with Bergson's opinion: since the soul can in certain circumstances act independently of the body, nothing obliges us to think that it must perish with the latter. And this probability can legitimately be deduced from *serious* experiments in parapsychology.

[4] THE SURVIVAL OF THE SOUL: AN OBJECT OF FAITH

The firm certainty with which most men profess the existence of a human soul as distinct from the body is not a matter, as we have said, of scientific knowledge. It is a matter of belief, of faith. It is psychologically quite understandable that at the beginning of the scientific era this mode of knowledge was rejected. The word "belief" was at that time considered a synonym for illusion and error. That age has gone. Today, even the most demanding scientists admit that scientific methods and techniques are far from able to disclose all of the real, that there are areas which elude them entirely by reason of the simple fact that they are not rational. In particular, ideas deriving from immediate experience cannot be demonstrated scientifically, for instance, our knowledge of our own real existence and that of the universe, as well as the immortality of the soul.

I shall take the liberty of referring once again to Jean Charon, whose position is all the more persuasive in that he does not, to my knowledge, belong to any church or organized religion and speaks purely as a scientist. "Man", he says, "is presently frustrated by his religious feelings, which are nonetheless necessary if he is to live an authentic life. He is frustrated by them because his Knowledge is not in harmony with his Faith. It is often said that Faith should change its language and adapt to Knowledge. But this is erroneous, because true Faith has no language. It is purely intuitive; it is what one feels and not what we can say about what we feel. Therefore, Knowledge must accommodate itself to Faith and not the contrary. Knowledge must, furthermore, accommodate itself to Metaphysics, and this the sciences of the last three centuries have resolutely refused to do. No doubt a non-metaphysical science can triumph over the empirical order, but this is not a human triumph because, beyond the empirical order, man is by nature a religious being, and religious because he 'feels' that he is infinitely more than Man and that this more belongs to a reality that is situated well beyond the empirical framework of things. . . . There is a kind of Knowledge which does not exclude Faith; and a kind of Faith that does not exclude Knowledge. Man needs this balance between his Knowledge and his Belief in order to 'live' humanly." (*L'Etre et le Verbe,* p. 270)

By "Knowledge," Charon means scientific knowledge. I would say that faith yields knowledge, although of an entirely different order. Otherwise, I am in perfect agreement with him.

The immortality of the soul is from all evidence, a matter of faith rather than science. As the eminent ethnologist, Sir James Frazer, wrote: "Life after death is not an object of speculation and conjecture among primitive peoples but rather of hope and fear. It is a practical certainty which the individual no more doubts than the reality of his conscious existence. He assumes it without inquiry and acts upon it as though it were, within the limits of human experience, one of the best established of truths." "Savages" bury and burn corpses and know that the body rots after death. Yet they regard the deceased as though he lives on. In India, as is well known, immortality is believed in with great certainty, and death is the object of the Buddha's revelations.

In the Christian West, for many centuries, death was not considered a mere biological event but as a specifically human reality. The Old French word for death, *trépas,* meant "passage," as did the Latin *decessus.* The later French term, *mort,* was used primarily in reference to those who were supposed to be damned. Moreover, even the sophisticated rationalist of today *does not experience* death, particularly his own death, as a simple biological fact. I have already alluded to those unbelievers who express extreme concern for their future burial.

It is evident, then, that man's faith in survival after death is in no way the fruit of philosophical speculation. The latter usually obscures our intuitive certitude of immortality. For twenty-five centuries the philosophers of the West have speculated on death and immortality, and this is undoubtedly why our faith in immortality is so riddled with doubt. Here again let me quote Jean Charon: ". . . Doesn't all the dynamism of the human adventure find its source in that permanent agony in the heart of Man? Could evolution pursue its course if we were satisfied, at ease, 'static'? True Faith is not the Faith of the 'washerwoman'; it is a Faith that doubts itself and relies on Man to aim higher than Man, toward an eternally inaccessible point." (*Ibid.,* p. 271)

Instead of asking those who believe in immortality to prove it, we might with equal justification ask those who do not believe to justify their unbelief "scientifically." It is pointless for the two sides to throw the ball of *onus probandi* back and forth, because we are dealing here with a matter that cannot be proven. The philosopher Max Scheler wrote: "I believe in the immortality of the soul because I have no reason to admit the contrary, and the *essential* conditions of what I believe are satisfied." He took these "essential conditions" to be the fact that the life of the spirit becomes increasingly liberated as it transcends biological dependence.

Still, it is in order to ask why so many educated men today not only doubt the immortality of the soul but deny it categorically. Perhaps the explanation lies in the fact that faith must express itself in "borrowed language" since intuition by definition is not conceptual. The naive beliefs of a prescientific age obviously cannot satisfy man in a scientific age. It is unfortunate for the cause of faith that believers perceived this divorce between faith and reason too late. Otherwise they might have formulated their faith in a way that could satisfy the educated man of today.

Zozima, in Dostoevsky's *The Brothers Karamazov,* was quite right when he accused Western civilization of uncritically rejecting all that is not rational, thus reducing man's capacity to love truly, since spontaneous belief in immortality is intimately related to love. "As your love grows," he said, "you will become more convinced of God's existence and the immortality of the soul."

[5]   SPIRITUAL EVOLUTION

Although some disproportion between faith and rational language is inevitable, we must make an attempt to translate the immediate postulates of consciousness into the language of intelligence. I am of the opinion that the concept of spiritual evolution, as elaborated by Teilhard de Chardin and his followers, is best suited to present faith in the immortality of the soul in a manner acceptable to modern man.

For millions of years, the immense and complex process of evolution on our planet seems to have tended toward the emergence of spirit. It is inconceivable (outside of an absurdist perspective) that this long preparation could end in pure and simple nothingness. It is, scientists say, one of the fundamental laws of the universe that what is possible must realize itself. The spirit's survival beyond corporeal disintegration thus appears to be fundamentally demanded by evolutionary creation. It is said that an evolutionary theory is optimistic. It would, indeed, be the darkest pessimism to think that what has been the goal of evolution, namely the spirit, must be extinguished in death like the flickering flame of a candle. This would be the only instance in which an evolutionary process was destructive instead of creative. When life appeared on earth, matter was not destroyed; nor will man's accession to the noosphere bring the biosphere to an end.

Obviously, I do not accept the thesis dear to Platonism (and even more so to neoplatonism) which asserts that union with the body is a punishment for the soul. I have insisted all along that the history of the spirit is inseparable from the history of matter. Because of matter the spirit was formed, evolved and acquired its capacity for full development. Teilhard de Chardin thinks that the spirit was not created or born spontaneously with man, but that it was virtually present in the more rudimentary forms of life. But its reign, the noosphere, began with man. However faithful a servant of the spirit we admit matter to be, there is a point beyond which it can no longer favor the activity and development of spirit because of its inherent limitations. It becomes in fact, an obstacle. We are made dramatically aware of this in the aging process. Sickness and infirmity overcome us; the body grows weaker and less able to support the spirit's activity.

Thus it seems to me in keeping with the known laws of evolution to suppose that when the life of the body ceases, the spirit is re-energized and capable of attaining a new level of evolution. Moreover, the body is not, strictly speaking, annihilated by death. It disintegrates; the matter that composed it continues to exist in other forms, whether animate or inanimate. It seems that at the root of all belief in metempsychosis, so widespread in the Orient and even in certain circles in the West, is an inadequate understanding of the originality and autonomy of the spirit. Since the matter which constitutes man's body can change into animal and vegetable forms of life, it is assumed that the same is true of the spiritual soul.

Teilhard de Chardin's comrades in the war of 1914–15 tell of his extraordinary courage in the face of danger. When they warned him to be careful, the young Jesuit replied, "Why should I be afraid of death since it is only a mutation, a mere change in state?" Probably unconsciously, he made his own, the words of Leibniz which I quoted in the beginning of this chapter, as well as those of Lamartine, who said, "To die is not to die but to change." Teilhard had already articulated what would be the core of his later philosophical and scientific work.

A basic intuition, therefore, teaches us that, for man, death does not represent a definitive end but a mutation, albeit the most important of all changes that take place in the course of a lifetime. Many authors establish a parallel between death and that other important transformation which is birth. The passage from the womb to the exterior world constitutes a veritable revolution in the condition of man. Depth psychology rightly speaks of a birth trauma that often results from this sudden change. From security and well-being in the mother's womb, the child comes into a world that is full of threats and insecurity, yet the change resulting from birth is not nearly so fundamental as that effected by death. There is no radical difference in the child's *being* before and after birth. There is only a simple, although very important, change in the conditions of his existence. On the other hand, the change effected by death concerns man's very essence. He is transported beyond the dimension of space and time which constitutes the very stuff of existence on earth. It is not empirical man who is immortal, but the spiritual principle in him.

There is nothing surprising in the fact that our senses cannot grasp life beyond the tomb. Even in our temporal condition, spiritual reality is always "invisible."

However radical the mutation brought about by death, I do not think we should consider it a total rupture with the world. Spirit is present in the whole of man—his thought, his emotions and his action. And men have always believed that the dead are capable of more-or-less permanent, more-or-less intense relationships with the living. We must, of course, place no credence in stories about ghosts, haunted houses and ouija boards. But enlightened believers are convinced that communication between the living and the dead is possible, at least through prayer.

Let us return to the analogy between birth and death. The child is certainly very much at ease in that haven of security which is his mother's womb. He would no doubt remain there forever if he could. But he can only actualize his human potential by changing states, by confronting the risks of birth and the struggles of life in the world. There is an analogical similarity to the case of the spirit and corporeal death. The spirit is accustomed to life with the material body through whose instrumentality it has found fulfillment. Naturally, it does not want to leave. However, to realize its destiny as spirit, to reach a level of superior existence, it must transcend this association with the body. "It is in dying that we are born," said Franklin. The Catholic martyrology calls the day of death *dies natalis,* the day of birth.

We might say with Lorenzo the Magnificent and Goethe that "those who do not believe in another life are already dead to this one." They are already dead because everything they undertake is mortal. "I do not doubt," Goethe wrote in 1829, "that there is life in the hereafter because it is in the order of nature that an entelechy cannot disappear." This is in perfect accord with Teilhard's vision. Goethe adds: "But we are not all immortal in the same way. If a man is to be an entelechy in the future he must first of all be one in this life." I agree fully with this idea and will develop it further in my last chapter. There is in fact a very real continuity between what a man is in his spatiotemporal existence and what he will be in life after death.

I do not think it can be disputed that man is more than his material body, that a part of him transcends the empirical order even in this life, that he is destined to survive the dissolution of the body. But it remains difficult to clarify the nature of this spiritual soul we speak of. By the force of things, its reality cannot be grasped by our senses, which are oriented to the existential while spirit by its very nature pertains to the order of being, of essence. All philosophical and theological definitions are merely analogical approximations. Personally, I find Aristotle's definition, despite its vagueness, quite acceptable: the soul is the spark of immortality in man.

In the immanent order of our universe, the highest degree of evolution is personal existence. Now, the individual becomes a person by reason of his spiritual soul. The most evolved animals have a certain degree of individuality, but they can never accede to personal existence. Hope in immortality results from the spiritual activity of man; it is a primordial requirement of an authentically personal life. As Louis Lavelle puts it: "The spiritual life is a moment-by-moment victory over death. It is entrance from this life into eternal life." It follows that the more authentic we are as persons and the more spiritually alive we are, the more immortality will seem to us one of those basic truths that need no rational proof. I would readily agree with Gabriel Marcel: "To consent to the final death of a single person would be in some sense to condemn him to death."

The survival of the spirit after empirical death raises a number of difficult problems. There is no question about that. But as the famous Viennese psychologist, Victor Frankl, put it so well, it is neither more nor less mysterious than the spirit's initial appearance in the universe. From a strictly scientific point of view, we can say nothing about the survival of the human soul. All the scientist can do is admit that he is up against realities that are inaccessible to his techniques.

We are here confronted with an enigma, a mystery. But all of existence, even in its spatiotemporal form, is a mystery as soon as we leave the surface of things and look into them more deeply. Science can tell us nothing about the origin of the soul and still less about its ultimate destiny. But it can tell us little more about the origin of the universe, the appearance of life on our planet and other less complex questions. This remark is not intended to discredit science. Its achievements are impressive and each of its conquests testifies to the power of the spirit. But man's spirit is not all-powerful and each science has its limitations and particular work to do.

The psychologist is also a scientist and can state that only eternal and personal survival can satisfy the deepest exigencies of man's heart and reason and give meaning to our life, the life of mankind, and the long and complex history of universal evolution. Teilhard de Chardin expresses my thought well: "The radical vice of all forms of faith in progress, such as those expressed in positivistic symbols, is not to have definitively eliminated death." Faith in immortality, far from conflicting with faith in progress, demands it and emanates from it. Death does not end progress but marks a new phase and form of progress. In this perspective, even if the human race as a whole should one day perish, progress would not be finally halted; millions of years of evolution and human creativity cannot end on an absurd note.

Thus there is nothing pejoratively individualistic or egocentric about our faith in the immortality of man's soul. It is the crowning glory of all who are endowed with spirit. Immortality is simply the ultimate conclusion of the irreversibility of universal evolution. "I realized that the discovery of an emerging spirit in myself and around me was nothing if that same spirit were not immortal," wrote Teilhard de Chardin in *How I Believe*. And he added, "That the universe *as a whole* will never stop or regress in the movement that draws it toward greater freedom and consciousness, is first of all suggested by the very nature of spirit. . . . There is in fact no recognizable limit to the depths of knowledge and love."

VII

Images of the Beyond

All I feel is an immense curiosity.
—LÉON BLOY

I HAVE not tried to *prove* that man's soul is immortal. But I do not think that faith in the survival of the soul, which I share with the majority of men, is an absurd illusion, a simple projection of a vain desire not to return to nothingness. Only this belief—or, if you prefer, this hypothesis—can give meaning to our lives and to a universe in a state of evolutionary creation.

The almost universal belief in the immortality of the human soul, however, yields an unsatisfactory certitude. We inevitably raise questions about how we will survive. And it goes without saying that psychology, in common with the other sciences, can have no direct access to what lies beyond death. It must be content to investigate the different beliefs and examine their degree of conformity with the exigencies of spiritual evolution, a doctrine that I accept because it satisfies both my heart and my reason better than any other explanation of the universe.

[I]   EXPERIENCES OF THE BEYOND

It would be normal for the psychologist, in investigating what lies beyond death, to address himself to those who claim to have had a direct experience with the Beyond. In the preceding chapter we examined the reliability of mediums concerning immortality. I think it would be more interesting to ask those who say they have communicated with the deceased what they have learned about the condition and modalities of immortal life. I have heard many spiritualists and mediums; I have attended some of their seances and read many of their books. Thus I want to approach this very delicate subject with as little prejudice as possible and deal exclusively with what is most valuable in these experiences, rather than drawing the easy but superficial conclusion that most spiritualists are obvious charlatans.

Here is the case of a mother whose only son died when he was sixteen. Her sorrow was so great that she lost all interest in living. Then one evening, while she was prostrate in bed, she suddenly had an unmistakable awareness of his presence. He told her that he was indescribably happy "in heaven" and begged her not to weep. These visits took place regularly and the woman lived for them. She was no longer unhappy and felt that her son was closer to her now than when he was alive. She began to take a renewed interest in life and, although a lukewarm believer before, became a fervent churchgoer. But these conversations between a mother and her son unfortunately tell us nothing about life after death. They consist almost solely in sentimental talk about the deceased's happiness and desire for future reunion with his mother in heaven. It goes without saying that the beneficiary of these communications with the "Beyond" is perfectly sincere. But the depth psychologist can scarcely be blamed if he accords no objective value to them. In his eyes everything transpires in the unhappy mother's psyche; her unconscious mind speaks to her in the name of her departed son.

One day I received a visit from an elderly and dignified gentleman, a jeweller by profession. He was a German Jew and had successfully fled his country with his family in 1936. Two years later he asked his youngest son to go clandestinely to Leipzig to get some jewels he had hidden in a safe place. His son was arrested by the Gestapo, sent to a death camp and was later killed. The father blamed himself for his son's death and was inconsolable. He had no interest whatever in his business. Wasn't it his love of money that had motivated him to send his son into the arms of the enemy? Some of his close friends recommended that he contact a well known "medium" in order to learn the exact fate of his son. The medium in question is in no sense of the word a charlatan. A highly educated woman and author of several books on parapsychological phenomena, she succeeded, by virtue of an extreme concentration which she said she had learned from Hindu ascetics, in entering into a kind of ecstatic trance during which she was convinced that she could communicate with the souls of the dead. The jeweller's son "appeared" to her. He expressed deep affection for his parents, begged his father not to blame himself for his death and to pursue his business concerns without a guilty conscience. He also spoke of his great happiness. By joining hands with the medium the father also *felt* the comforting presence of his son. He did not hear his voice but heard him speak "to his heart." This sceptical man, without the least predisposition to illuminations of this sort, was firmly convinced of the objectivity of the experience

and found a new joy in living. He was a man of action, ruth-
less in business matters and only minimally religious. I recommended that he ask his medium to put precise questions
about life in the Beyond to his son. The answers, unfortunately, were far from satisfactory. The only thing we learned
is that one is very happy "there," that the deceased are intensely involved in the earthly life of their loved ones, that
they see and hear everything that goes on here below. Here
again, the psychologist cannot avoid the impression that the
medium, whose good faith we have no reason to doubt, is
communicating more with the jeweller's unconscious than
with his dead son.

There has been much discussion in the past fifty years about
the moving writings and high spirituality of Mme Marcelle
de Jouvenel. I have no intention of judging the authenticity
of the "messages" she is reputed to have received from the
Beyond. Nor do I want to cast suspicion on those (and there
are many of them) who attribute these beautiful writings to
"revelations" made by the dead. Among those who fervently
believe in them are men of high culture and intense spiritual
life. What I personally look for in these writings is some
information about the Beyond with which Mme Jouvenel
and other such authors are supposed to communicate. I have
learned nothing new from them. Supposing that the "voices"
really came from the Beyond—and not the mysterious depths
of the personal or collective unconscious of those who hear
them—we could only be sure about one thing: namely, that
the deceased can in some way share in the lives of the living.

As is well known, accounts of communication with the
dead abound in the traditions of every nation and every
religion. In primitive societies the role of the medium is filled

by sorcerers who are revered and feared by their people. The Old Testament, for example, relates among other analogous facts King Saul's nocturnal visit to the pythoness which, despite legal interdictions, was known for her power of evoking the dead who were reputed to know how the future would affect the living. At the king's request, the pythoness summoned the prophet Samuel who predicted Saul's defeat in the near future. But here again, the dead tell us nothing about themselves. The only thing we can legitimately deduce from such "apparitions" of the dead is that they are not reduced to nothingness and have at their disposal a power and a knowledge that is far superior to those of the living.

But one fact deserves special mention: The voices from beyond always speak in the religious and philosophical language of their earthly interlocutors. The deceased son of the Catholic Marcelle de Jouvenel utters beautiful exhortations in the best tradition of Catholic mysticism. The Protestant, Jew and Moslem receive messages in which they can find confirmation of their own religious beliefs. We might suppose that a Communist medium—if the party authorized such— would enter into the spirit of Lenin, and Marxist orthodoxy would also be sanctioned by the Beyond. Do those who believe in such "revelations" think that there is a special Beyond for each human category? It seems to me more reasonable to think that, on the hypothesis that there is true communication with the deceased, each medium expresses in his own intellectual or emotional language an experience that is objectively ineffable.

We need not discuss further the supposed communication with the dead by means of ouija boards and the like. Either these are mere tricks, of the kind practiced by magicians in circuses, or those who hear voices are endowed with a psychic power that for want of a better name I would call "magnetic." Usually this sort of communication lacks the seriousness that characterizes the kind of medium we have been talking about in this chapter.

The Gospels report three instances of resurrection from the dead. These reports are of special interest to the Christian. Unfortunately, neither the centurion's daughter nor the widow of Naïm's son seem to have said anything about their experiences of death. Modern exegetes conclude that in all probability neither was really dead. Thus, these are cases of miraculous cure rather than resurrection in the strict sense of the word. Then there is the case of Jesus' friend, Lazarus of Bethany. Since he had been buried for three days it seems likely that his death was real. Had he said anything about his death the evangelists, who knew him personally, would undoubtedly have recorded it. According to legend, Lazarus lived a long time after the Passion and is said to have become the first bishop of Marseille. It is interesting that the legend reports nothing relative to his experience of death.

Thus we can learn nothing about the state of souls after death from either those who have claimed to communicate with the dead or those who are supposed to have been raised from the dead. Some mystics say they have had a foretaste of heavenly beatitude in ecstasy. But they admit that human language cannot translate their experience. As St. Paul wrote to the Corinthians: "I know a man in Christ, who, fourteen years ago, whether in or out of the body, I know not but God knoweth, was caught up to the third heaven. . . . That he was caught up into paradise and heard *ineffable words* which it is not granted to man to utter." (II Corinthians 12:2–3) Theresa of Avila and other mystics do not satisfy our curiosity any more than Paul. We can only conclude that eternity is beyond the empirical order to which our senses, language and concepts are adapted.

Dante's *The Divine Comedy* offers a detailed narrative of the life of the deceased in heaven, hell and purgatory. There is good evidence for believing that Dante was trying to communicate a mystic experience in his poem. But his inner experience is so rigorously confined by the language of scholastic theology that we learn nothing *concrete* about the condition of the dead. Once again we are confronted with the problem of the inadequacy of our language to express transphenomenal realities, a problem which since Bergson's time has been the object of many scholarly studies by both philosophers and scientists.

[2]   GREEN PASTURES

Several years ago an American film of this title enjoyed great success, in Europe as well as America. It portrayed biblical history and particularly paradise, the resting place of the blessed, as seen through the eyes of an American Negro. I do not know whether or not the authors of this film were influenced by Feuerbach's theories on the origins of the religious sentiment as a projection into the beyond of man's frustrated desires in this world. But I got the distinct impression that the film expressed the psychological truth of a deprived class. On the basis of the evidence, the Negro conception of religion was a movingly naive projection of their frustrations. They read the Bible as though it were their own immediate history rather than that of the Jewish people several thousand years ago. The walls of Jericho fell before *their* eyes and permitted *them* to see the green pastures of Canaan, the symbol of Paradise, the land God promised to those he loves. The joys hoped for were not particularly "spiritual." They rather resembled the pleasures which the inhabitants of Harlem and other Negro ghettos imagine are enjoyed by the rich.

Contemporary militant atheism, in almost all of its forms, follows the nineteenth-century German philosopher, Ludwig Feuerbach, in accounting for the origin of religious faith, particularly faith in the beyond. We might summarize as follows what Marxism, Freudian psychoanalysis and atheistic existentialism say about the question of the immortality of the soul: Man's life on earth has always been highly disproportionate to his aspirations. He has always been deprived and frustrated; hunger, sickness, old age, death and countless other misfortunes darken the joy of life. But in his heart every man wants to be happy. He dares not hope that he can attain this happiness by his own strength. As soon as he achieves what once represented happiness for him, his heart desires something else. Morever, man cannot renounce his desires and aspirations. In order to prevent his inability to satisfy his deep desire for happiness from plunging him into irremediable despair, he has only one recourse and that is to project the satisfaction of all his desires beyond death. Faith in God and everything that constitutes religion, especially belief in an afterlife, is therefore, according to Feuerbach and his followers, a myth spontaneously created by the human psyche. If man were not frustrated by unfulfilled desires, he would have no need of God or an afterlife. Men dare not hope that knowledge, love, power and justice can be realized by them on earth. Yet they cannot do without these values and consequently project them beyond the empirical order and hope to enjoy just enough of them in this life to give them a foretaste of that plenitude reserved for life after death. The logical consequence of this theory is that the more perfect a religion, the more alienated are those who believe in it. This is what Marx, Freud, Sartre and other leading exponents of atheism derive from Feuerbach. That is why, too, they take it upon themselves to oppose Christianity, which they generally recognize as objectively superior to other religions.

This is not the place to discuss the philosophical and theological merits of the projection theory. It is evident that a Christian theologian must reject such a concept of the Beyond. But we may inquire into the psychological worth of this theory. The psychologist, who has had ample opportunity to observe the behavior of Christians and other believers, must admit that the theoretical projection of frustrated desires is no mere speculative invention of Hegel's disciples. For the most part, it is borne out by our daily experience.

The crudest and most obvious example of this projection seems to be furnished by Islamic imagery, much like that of "Green Pastures." The Moslem paradise, according to the Koran, resembles a rich oasis as desert nomads in frequent encounters with hunger, thirst and heat might imagine it. In this paradisical oasis water flows in abundance, and the occupants partake of delicious foods in a cooling shade. For all of eternity men will enjoy the services of the most voluptuous and beautiful women, who will always be young and virginal. One does not have to be a depth psychologist to recognize in such images of the beyond the projection of frustrated desires. We need only recall the conditions under which the

Arabs of Mohammed's time lived, and in many cases still live, to realize that the promises of this religion correspond rather directly to the unfulfilled aspirations of its adherents.

[3] THE CHRISTIAN PARADISE

The original Christian concept of heaven was more purified and appreciably more subtle and less materialistic than that of the Moslems. The more educated Christian believers became, the less their representations of the Beyond gave the impression of being projections of frustrated desires. Even the ascetics did not seem to feel frustrated; thus they had nothing to project. Too, in many so-called Christian countries, material frustration and alienation are decreasing, and technology promises to eliminate what remains. Therefore, the hope of satisfying our needs is less frequently projected to the Beyond.

The relative prosperity of the West today should not make us forget that for centuries the Christian people lived in great privation. Even today in South America and Southern Europe many Christians live in material and moral misery. Survival is a day-to-day struggle for them. Too, wars and revolutions are a constant threat to international and social peace. Even the most privileged are victims of illness and anxiety. Is it not in some sense symptomatic of the human condition that the modern philosophers of despair flourish less in South America, Spain and Portugal (not to mention Africa and Asia) than in Europe and North America? It seems that when material alienation decreases, spiritual and moral alienation increases.

Given these conditions, it is not surprising that many Christians also envisage "heaven" as a place of "eternal rest."

There, one presumably finds rest from all fear and anxiety in contemplating God and, as popular faith would have it, in singing hymns of praise to Christ, the Blessed Virgin and the saints. In a public lecture I once remarked, quite incidentally, that Christ did not promise us eternal rest but *eternal life* and that the concept of "life" is scarcely synonymous with "rest." Many in the audience were troubled and did not understand. Many men are in fact weary of life, and the thought of a life in the fullest sense of the word is no cause for them to rejoice.

Since Christ taught the divine sonship of all men, Christianity is quite naturally more sensitive than other religions to social injustices. That the "wicked" are often more endowed with the goods of this world than the "good" is a scandal that the Christian conscience finds difficult to accept, even though it is common knowledge that the good and the wicked do not constitute two distinct human categories. Rather, good and evil are inextricably commingled in our hearts. Unlike the Jews of Biblical times and modern Marxists, both of whom hope for the reign of absolute justice on this earth, Christians engaged in the struggle for social justice doubt that it can ever be perfect. Thus it is in the logic of Christian belief to represent "heaven" primarily as the reign of that justice toward which we aspire but which seems unlikely to be fully realized on earth. Christians sometimes fall prey to the temptation to abandon the struggle for justice here below and project their aspirations to the beyond.

Nor is this totally unwarranted by Scripture. The prophets of the Old Testament preached that the restoration of the order willed by God would take place in a future messianic reign. A number of evangelical parables explicitly encourage such projections—although less crudely than the Koran.

Christ himself compared the "kingdom of heaven" to a wedding feast. And Lazarus entered into the bosom of Abraham after his death while the wicked rich man suffered in hell. To be sure, enlightened Christians interpret the evangelical parables as allegories intended to communicate spiritual truths. But we should not be surprised if simple men take them literally. The more so since the Church herself long insisted on the literal truth of the scriptures.

A certain kind of simple-minded atheism accuses the founders and ministers of different religions of deliberately deceiving the people. They promise happiness in another life so the people will resign themselves to their sorry lot in this life and let the privileged few enjoy temporal prosperity. There is no doubt that there have been scandalous abuses in this respect. But such abuses do not fully account for the psychological truth of projection. Karl Marx, who did not hesitate to denounce the bad influence of religious projections on the revolutionary struggle for the reign of justice and universal fraternity on earth, was a much better psychologist than many of his disciples. Long before the birth of modern depth psychology, the projection of frustrated desires was recognized as an expression of a universal psychological faculty. And this mechanism was as evident in atheists as believers. However "scientific" Marxist communism claims to be, its promise of a classless society, absolutely egalitarian and just, derives from exactly the same psychological process as the Jewish expectation of a messianic kingdom (where the lamb and the lion would lie down together), the Islamic paradise and the more popular Christian images of the kingdom of heaven. From a psychological point of view, it matters little whether the frustrated desires of men are projected beyond time or to a distant future on earth. In both cases it is a question of an imaginary satisfaction of frustrated desires. In both cases satisfaction in the future serves as a compensation for a present state of alienation. Marx understood full well that religion was less a conscious machination of "the knavish valets of capitalism" than a spontaneous psychic function. We might add that this projection mechanism acts unconsciously.

Perhaps men would renounce such projections if all of their desires were satisfied. But this is only a theoretical possibility, for new desires would arise as soon as the old ones had been fulfilled. As we see clearly in our modern consumer society, frustrations are increasing rather than diminishing. The poor peasant in India is apparently less frustrated than the citizens of Stockholm or Zurich. Wouldn't the absence of desire, and therefore the need of projection, spell the end of human progress? It seems to me that Hegel was right to consider man's many desires as the distinctive sign of his humanity. This is what enables him to evolve and constitutes his superiority to other animals.

[4] ETERNAL LIFE

In the light of the foregoing it would be vain and unjust to condemn the need for projection in the human psyche in the name of "realism." I am inclined to think that this need, or capacity, on occasion plays an altogether existentially positive role. Moreover, we have no basis for affirming that our projected images of the beyond are absolutely illusory. We may very legitimately suppose that the reason man's desires and aspirations are so great that all progress only increases them is precisely that human reality must find its fulfillment beyond space and time. The laws which govern man's desires do not seem to be very different from those which govern instincts. And every instinct has a corresponding object. Would it then be so very "anti-scientific" to think that for all our desires, especially our basic desire for happiness, there is a possibility of adequate satisfaction? The only thing that might be questioned is the mediocre quality of the desires most men expect to be fulfilled in the hereafter. We can readily dismiss the pious image of heaven given by many catechisms. We would be bored to death in such a place.

The more man evolves in the noosphere, the more spiritual are his needs. Now, since man's spirit enters into eternal life, it is perfectly logical to suppose that the projections of men of greater spiritual maturity will be closer to the truth than those of men whose desires are for the most part sensual. Let us admit, on the basis of what was said in the preceding chapter, that the hypothesis of immortality, if not "proven," is at least in conformity with the laws that seem to regulate universal growth. There is no doubt that the man whose existential frustration is due to the inadequacy of his capacities to know and love has a much greater chance of finding his desires satisfied in the beyond than the man whose frustrations are of the material order.

But we must also admit that if the survival of the spiritual soul is in perfect conformity with the immanent logic of a universe in evolution—an evolution tending toward an increasingly perfect state of spiritualization—we have no way of knowing with certainty in just what this immortality consists. The so-called direct experiences of spiritualists and mediums tell us nothing. Books of revelations are extremely discreet on this subject. And projections of frustrated desires —however "spiritual" they may be—are at best analogies. We have every right to hope that eternal life will fulfill us, but we do not know how.

This difficulty is not surprising. Even in the immanent order of our universe we are scarcely able to imagine, what, for example, the political and economic state of Europe will be in the year 2500. How, then, can we imagine Eternity?

But we may profitably meditate upon some of the fundamental themes of the universe in evolution and upon what we take to be the most characteristic constituent of spiritual reality. At this level our meditation should be both psychological and religious, because it is impossible to talk about eternal life without reference to religion.

I understand eternal life to be the fulfillment rather than the destruction of temporal life. Let me insist once again that, contrary to some pious formulations, the doctrine under discussion here refers to eternal *life* and not rest. It is understandable, from a psychological point of view, that men who are old or tired of life might find the prospect of eternal rest attractive. But those who love the risks and opportunities for creation that life offers quite normally aspire for something other than repose. In my opinion, the latter are right. The old and tired, however, might take consolation in the thought that only the body is subject to age and wear; in eternity they will live more intensely than they ever did on earth. Contrary to their claims, those who deny eternal life do not really love life, for it is the nature of all love to want to be eternal.

All the evidence indicates that the most specifically spiritual human activities are knowledge and love. We become *more human* not by producing or consuming more but by developing our faculties of knowing and loving. It is therefore normal to suppose that knowledge and love will constitute the essential activities of eternal life. There is no danger that these activities will ever become boring. Those who have experienced authentic love and intellectual achievement know well that they can never reach a saturation point. The scientist who consecrates all of his time and energy to research knows that the more he learns, the more there is to learn and the more his appetite for knowledge increases. Likewise, those who love truly know that there is no imaginable limit to the growth of their love. And in eternity there will be no obstacles to our appetite for knowledge and love.

Not everyone will enjoy eternal life in the same degree. Those who in this life live at a slower pace and make but modest use of their faculties of knowing and loving will have a proportionate share in eternal life. On the other hand, the *passionate,* those who love and seek truth with enthusiasm and perseverance will continue to grow throughout eternity. The idea of progress is in fact so intimately related to that of life that we can only conceive of eternal life as eternal growth. It is in this sense that we must interpret the evangelical parable concerning the many mansions in the kingdom of heaven. There is no injustice in this kind of inequality; it is in perfect conformity with the fundamental laws of life, whether temporal or eternal. Still, our human concepts represent eternal life very inadequately. In whatever "mansion" the human spirit finds itself and whatever its rhythm of growth, it will necessarily be fulfilled. We might recall here the image of the vases. Although of different sizes, they are all equally full. So it will be with souls in eternity; each will grow at its own pace and always be fulfilled.

Must we believe, have we any right to hope, that our participation in eternal life will be personal? It is a well known fact that the most deeply religious peoples—practically all of the Orient—are pantheistic. And pantheism conceives of immortality as the dissolution of the individual in the cosmic (or divine) Whole.

When I analyze my own spiritual aspirations no part of

me has ever objected to pantheism. From a purely psychological point of view I could easily be a pantheist. I have long believed in eternal life. I don't think any "argument" could shake that faith. But the desire "to save my soul" plays little role in my faith. For a long period in my youth I lived without either religious faith or metaphysical anguish. I don't think I ever asked myself what would become of me after death. My life would be amply justified if I could make some contribution to the present and future welfare of the human community. Later, my experiences of life, reflection and meditation led me to realize that my efforts (and the efforts of all men) would not be worth much in the long run if they did not contribute somehow to the creation of something eternal. But my sensitivity in no way required that this eternal work be my own individuality. It could well be a Whole in which all individual consciousness would dissolve. When I converted to Christianity I was of course conscious of myself as an individual, but I was more conscious of my appurtenance to the Whole. The doctrine of the Mystical Body played a determining role in my conversion to Catholicism, rather than to another Christian church, and I was quite disposed to interpret this doctrine in a pantheistic sense. It was only much later, principally because of Teilhard de Chardin's influence, that I really became conscious of myself as a *person*.

Today I believe in personal immortality as a result of meditating on universal evolution. It is, as we have seen, virtually impossible to predict with any precision the modalities of the future state of the universe and that microcosm which is man. Nonetheless, when the different scientific disciplines have determined what the universal laws of evolution were for the past, we may suppose that those same laws will apply to the future course of evolution. The work of Teilhard de Chardin and other eminent scientists has demonstrated that our universe has always tended, despite rather serious relapses, toward greater spiritualization. Moreover, the supreme degree of spiritualization is realized in the constitution of the person. "The personalized being," Teilhard de Chardin wrote, "that makes us *human* is the highest state in which we are able to grasp the stuff of the world. The dead man can only be super-conscious, super-personal. . . . It is impossible to conceive of an evolution toward the spirit which would not end in a supreme personality. . . . In a naturally evolutionary universe, the existence of spirit necessarily excludes the possibility of a death in which the conquests of the spirit would disappear *totally*."

The law which demands that man die as an individual also demands that he subsist as a person. If it were not thus, man would be a lamentable failure instead of the supreme achievement of the evolutionary process. What essentially constitutes man is his spiritual soul and this, therefore, is what will survive.

The East believes in metempsychosis, reincarnation. Many Western men, following Schopenhauer and Nietzsche, think they can overcome the difficulties that faith in personal immortality poses to our reason by professing the Eastern belief. But in reality this only shifts the grounds of the problem, since Orientals themselves believe that they will one day attain a degree of purification sufficient to enable them to attain final salvation. Moreover, many specialists today think that the Hindu belief in metempsychosis results from a popular corruption of the mystical doctrine of spiritual ascent taught in the Upanishads, a doctrine analogous to *The Ascent of Mount Carmel* by Saint John of the Cross. A well known Hindu writer has pointed out that there is nothing to prevent a Christian from believing in reincarnation, that no explicit teaching of the ecclesiastical magisterium condemns such a doctrine. This may be the case, but it does nothing to solve the problem under consideration here. Whether the soul is united to the body once or a thousand times comes to the same thing in the end. Still, I find it surprising that a man like Nietzsche, who exalted the tragic dimension of life, did not understand that a belief which accorded man but one chance to realize all his potentiality emphasizes the tragic character of human existence better than doctrines of metempsychosis or pantheism.

Whatever the credibility of the doctrines of reincarnation, if we do not survive our empirical death as persons, then the whole long process of evolution is inexplicable and absurd. The scientific perspective that supports my faith enables me to say that we will be saved from the corruption of death by virtue of that in us which is most authentically personal. It follows that any spiritual enrichment of our person during temporal existence is extremely important because it is destined to become an integral part of our eternity. Thus the way in which we live here below is directly relevant to our future state. In saying this, I am not thinking primarily of the moral doctrine that urges us to avoid sin and accumulate merit. I am thinking rather of the intensity and depth of our lives. From the point of view of eternity, there is a big difference between a life spent uselessly and one which realizes to the maximum our potential for knowledge and love. There is something false in the "mysticism" of detachment and humility that has been so important in the history of Christian spirituality, a mysticism which taught that to build cathedrals or peel apples came to the same thing since neither the cathedrals nor the apples would enter the kingdom of God; our intentions alone determine the objective worth of what we do. In the perspective we have adopted here, the objective, temporal value of what we do in this life has great importance for eternal life. The more we develop our faculties of knowledge and love, the more they will contribute to the fulfillment of our personality, and the more intensely will we be able to participate in eternal life. "From the very heart of my indifference to immortality springs its necessity," wrote Teilhard de Chardin.

This highly personalized conception of immortality should not, however, be conceived as an exaltation of individualism or a negation of the communitarian nature of eternal life. Man's individualization has ruptured or at least relaxed his ties to the community, but his growth as a person implies the recuperation of the communitarian reality. All of Emmanuel Mounier's philosophical work elaborates a clear distinction between personalism and individualism, and urges a revolution that would be at once personalist and communitarian. And by that token it is in the most fundamental Christian tradition. The pantheist and pancosmic doctrines of the Orient more or less explicitly conceive of immortality as a return to the pre-individual undifferentiatedness of primitive societies. Our conception of immortality does not imply the destruction of either the person or the community but the supreme fulfillment of both.

One of the most pointless questions those who do not believe in immortality ask believers—but which also occurs to the latter—bears on the *location* of the souls of the deceased. In the fourth century the great Christian thinker of Capodocia, Gregory of Nyssa, already understood that the concept of eternity must be stripped of all spatial and temporal imagery. Eternity is not immobile time. While time knows only the past and future and basically ignores the present, eternity is a present without end and without limit. But this eternal present is not immobility, because beatitude consists in life rather than death.

Place pertains to the temporal mode of existence. Once they shed the material body, immortal spirits must also be freed from the limitations of space and time. It is understandably difficult to imagine a life that is not subject to the laws of space and time, since our present existence is entirely dependent upon such laws. However, space and time are not the constitutive stuff, but merely the conditions, of our existence.

Man's spirit, as we have noted, is freed from the material body in the transition to eternal life. But we should not for this reason conceive of it as a "pure spirit." Man's life, whether temporal and eternal, always seems to require a certain corporeal support. To make this clearer we can do no better than to quote St. Paul's words to the Corinthians: "But some man will say, How do the dead rise again? Or with what manner of body shall they come? Senseless man, that which thou sowest is not quickened, except it die first. And when thou sowest, thou sowest not the body that shall be, but the bare grain, of wheat or some other cereal. God giveth it a body as he will, and to every seed its proper body. All flesh is not the same flesh; there is the flesh of men, of beasts, of birds, of fishes. There are celestial bodies and terrestrial bodies, but one is the glory of the celestial, and another of the terrestrial. One is the glory of the sun, another the glory of the moon, and another the glory of the stars. For star differeth from star in glory. So also is the resurrection of the dead. It is sown in corruption; it shall rise in corruption. . . . It is sown a natural body; it shall rise a spiritual body. If there be a natural body there is also a spiritual body. . . . Yet that was not first which is spiritual, but that which is natural . . . afterwards that which spiritual." (I Corinthians 15:35–46)

It is quite remarkable that Paul of Tarsus, a student of the Jewish Pharisees, could write the lines I have just quoted in an age when the Platonic contempt for matter and the body as well as a static conception of the universe dominated the Hellenized world. What he wrote is in perfect agreement with our present evolutionist–transformist vision of reality.

In a spirit of fidelity to our global vision of the universe, and in agreement with St. Paul, we believe, then, that it is not only our souls but the total man who will live eternally. Due to the great mutation effected by death, the material body will simply be replaced by a "spiritual" body—or better still, a *spiritualized* body.